Epistemological Disjunctivism

'In his excellent book, *Epistemological Disjunctivism*, Duncan Pritchard embarks on a quest for the epistemological equivalent of the "Holy Grail"—an epistemological theory that combines the insights of internalism and externalism in such a way as to offer a new and more satisfying solution to the skeptical problem . . . The result is an original, sophisticated, and well-articulated position [. . . *written in a*] style which is clear, accessible, and engaging. In addition to making an original contribution to the contemporary literature, this book would be well suited for graduate and advanced undergraduate courses on the epistemology of perceptual knowledge; indeed, I have used it for this purpose myself . . . In conclusion, epistemological disjunctivism is a fascinating view that deserves critical scrutiny . . . Pritchard deserves credit for articulating this view so clearly and putting it on the agenda for discussion.'

Declan Smithies, Ohio State University,
in *Notre Dame Philosophical Reviews*

'Pritchard's discussion is a great success. Parts One and Two of the book succeed in answering widely held objections to the view, and Part Three demonstrates the view's significant advantages *vis-à-vis* an important kind of skepticism. Moreover, Pritchard's expositions of the position and his arguments in favour of it are remarkably lucid, no small task for a subject matter that often eludes clear treatment. In sum, Pritchard's book successfully brings epistemological disjunctivism to center stage as a theory of visual knowledge. Philosophers interested in perceptual knowledge and in replies to scepticism will have to take the position seriously, and Pritchard's book will have to be the starting place for doing so.'

John Greco, Saint Louis University, in *Philosophical Quarterly*

'There is so much to like (and so much to recommend) about *Epistemological Disjunctivism*. It is philosophically deep, with many subtle distinctions that I have not been able to do justice to in the overview given here. This subtlety does not come at the expense of clarity, though—the book is hugely readable from start to finish. Some of the most interesting philosophical discussion comes from taking a theory that is commonly taken to be obviously false and showing that the apparently obvious arguments against it fail. Pritchard's book does just this and it does so in a way that is fascinating, engaging and above all thought-provoking. There is much to be learned here.'

Stephen Wright, University of Sheffield, in *Dialectica*

'*Epistemological Disjunctivism* is original and insightful and I can recommend it without reservation...Hopefully, Pritchard's book will receive the careful consideration it deserves. If it does, it should have a tremendous impact on a number of recent debates in epistemology.'

Clayton Littlejohn, King's College London, in *Mind*

Epistemological Disjunctivism

Duncan Pritchard

OXFORD
UNIVERSITY PRESS

OXFORD
UNIVERSITY PRESS

Great Clarendon Street, Oxford, OX2 6DP,
United Kingdom

Oxford University Press is a department of the University of Oxford.
It furthers the University's objective of excellence in research, scholarship,
and education by publishing worldwide. Oxford is a registered trade mark of
Oxford University Press in the UK and in certain other countries

First Edition published in 2012
First published in paperback 2014

Published in the United States of America by Oxford University Press
198 Madison Avenue, New York, NY 10016, United States of America

British Library Cataloguing in Publication Data
Data available

Library of Congress Cataloging in Publication Data
Data available

ISBN 978-0-19-955791-2 (Hbk)
ISBN 978-0-19-870896-4 (Pbk)

For Mandi, Ethan, and Alexander

Contents

Acknowledgements

I have benefited greatly from discussing the topics covered in this book with colleagues. J. Adam Carter, Chris Kelp, Adrian Haddock, Scott Sturgeon, and three anonymous referees for Oxford University Press very helpfully read an early draft of the book and gave me detailed feedback, for which I am extremely grateful. For discussions on topics related to the book, special thanks go to Tony Brueckner, Stew Cohen, Pascal Engel, Sandy Goldberg, John Greco, Allan Hazlett, Jesper Kallestrup, Michael Lynch, John McDowell, Marie McGinn, Alan Millar, Ram Neta, Genia Schönbaumsfeld, Ernie Sosa, and Crispin Wright. Thanks also to Avery Archer, Michael Blome-Tillmann, Michael Brady, Berit Brogaard, Jessica Brown, Cameron Boult, Quassim Cassam, Andy Clark, Annalisa Coliva, James Conant, Earl Conee, Fabian Dorsch, Trent Dougherty, Antony Duff, Gary Ebbs, Richard Fumerton, Andrea Giananti, Clayton Littlejohn, Brent Madison, Fiona Macpherson, Conor McHugh, Jim Pryor, Christopher Ranalli, Martin Smith, David Sosa, Finn Spicer, Barry Stroud, Peter Sullivan, and John Turri. Peter Momtchiloff, and everyone else at Oxford University Press for that matter, was supportive and helpful throughout. Of course, despite all this sterling assistance, all my mistakes are entirely my own. Finally, this book owes a tremendous intellectual debt to the towering work of John McDowell.

Elements of this book have been presented at a number of venues. These include: a conference on *Contextualism* in Bled, Slovenia, in 2004; a conference on *Contextualism* at the Amsterdam Free University in 2004; a conference on *Disjunctivism* at the University of Glasgow in 2005; a conference on *Externalism and Internalism in Semantics and Epistemology* at the University of Kentucky in 2005; and departmental talks since 2005 at the following universities: Aarhus, Birmingham, Brown, Cambridge, Copenhagen, Edinburgh, Hull, Nottingham, Rijeka, St Andrews, and York.

As is common for a monograph, some of the ideas advanced here can be found in various forms in earlier articles. The basic idea that epistemological disjunctivism is a far more plausible position than many give it credit for can be found in a paper that I co-authored with Ram Neta: 'McDowell and the New Evil Genius', *Philosophy and Phenomenological Research* 74 (2007),

381–96. This idea was further explored in the specific context of the problem of radical scepticism in my 'McDowellian Neo-Mooreanism', *Disjunctivism: Perception, Action, Knowledge*, ed. A. Haddock and F. Macpherson, 283–310, Oxford: Oxford University Press, 2008. The general distinction between favouring and discriminating epistemic support that is central to part two of this book is developed in my 'Relevant Alternatives, Perceptual Knowledge and Discrimination', *Noûs* 44 (2010), 245–68. Finally, the issue of how epistemological disjunctivism deals with what I call the 'basis problem', a topic which is covered in part one of this book, is discussed in 'Epistemological Disjunctivism and the Basis Problem', *Philosophical Issues* 21 (2011), 434–55.

D. H. P.

Edinburgh, November 2011

Introduction

My interest is in a certain account of perceptual knowledge, what I will be calling *epistemological disjunctivism*.[1] Most epistemologists, when I sketch the view to them, tell me that it's *plainly* false. Indeed, when I first came across the view—more than a decade ago—I thought it was obviously wrong too. Over time, though, I've become convinced, bit by bit, that there is something in it and that it just might be right. Not much of a ringing endorsement for an idea, you might think. Why would one want to read a book—much less *write* a book—describing a view which the author concedes is a position that most informed people hold is obviously wrong and which even he will only claim 'might' be right? But it's not that simple.

This is because the view in question, if it were right, would represent the *holy grail* of epistemology. This may sound as if I am over-egging the matter, but let me see if I can convince you that this is not so. The most direct way of making the case for the radical import of epistemological disjunctivism is by laying out the challenge that it poses for one of the most central distinctions in contemporary epistemology—*viz.*, the distinction between epistemic externalism and epistemic internalism. The conventional wisdom has it that this distinction maps out an exclusive and exhaustive set of options: either one is an epistemic externalist or one is an epistemic internalist, and there is no third option available.[2] Notoriously, this debate between externalism and internalism in epistemology has long been stuck in an *impasse*, in that each side of the distinction seems to be answering to important epistemological considerations, such that to opt for either side of the distinction (as it seems one must) behoves one to give up on a significant epistemological insight.

On the one hand, epistemic internalism seems best placed to capture our intuitions about such key notions for epistemologists as epistemic responsibility. This is because it essentially connects an agent's epistemic standing to factors which are 'internal' to the agent, where this typically means factors that the agent has reflective access to. Put another way, epistemic internalism ensures that there is a significant degree of reflective *transparency* in the epistemic standing of our beliefs which makes it easier to make sense of how we could properly be held to account for those beliefs. Crucially, however, epistemic internalism faces a formidable drawback in that it struggles to show how the epistemic standing for our 'worldly' beliefs—e.g., beliefs about one's immediate physical environment—should bear any essential connection to the worldly facts that these beliefs are ostensibly about. In a nutshell, by internalist lights one can enjoy an excellent epistemic standing for one's worldly beliefs and yet it won't thereby follow that any of these beliefs are even likely to be true.[3]

In contrast, epistemic externalism doesn't face this problem at all, since on this view there is a very direct connection between the epistemic standing for our beliefs and the relevant 'worldly' facts which these beliefs concern. In particular, having a good epistemic standing for one's beliefs by externalist lights will actually *entail* certain facts about the world, such as facts about the reliability of the process by which the belief was acquired. But epistemic externalist positions attain this advantage by allowing that the epistemic standing of one's beliefs can be excellent even though one possesses very little (if anything) by way of reflectively accessible support for the target beliefs.

After all, facts about, say, the reliability of a subject's belief-forming processes are unlikely to be reflectively available to that subject, and yet on epistemic externalist views they can nonetheless be central to determining the epistemic standing of the beliefs formed by that subject via these processes. Put another way, epistemic externalism entails that there is a significant degree of reflective *opacity* in the epistemic standing of our beliefs. This generates a fundamental difficulty for epistemic externalist positions, which is that it is hard on this view to capture any adequate notion of epistemic responsibility. For if the facts in virtue of which one's beliefs enjoy a good epistemic standing are not reflectively available to one, then in what sense is one even able to take epistemic responsibility for that epistemic standing?

It is in the context of this *impasse* between epistemic externalism and internalism that epistemological disjunctivism offers such tremendous theoretical potential. Here, in sloganizing form, is the central claim of epistemological disjunctivism: perceptual knowledge is paradigmatically constituted by a true belief whose epistemic support is both factive (i.e., it entails the truth of the proposition believed) *and* reflectively accessible to the agent. (The reasons why the view is called 'epistemological disjunctivism' will become clearer in part one.)

Such a view seems to achieve the apparently impossible feat of incorporating key elements of both epistemic internalism and externalism (at least as regards the domain of perceptual knowledge). From epistemic internalism it takes the idea that knowledge demands epistemic support that is reflectively available to the subject. In doing so it is in a position to capture, in line with standard forms of epistemic internalism, the role that epistemic responsibility plays in our acquisition of (perceptual) knowledge. From epistemic externalism it takes the idea that knowledge requires an objective connection between the epistemic support for our beliefs and the relevant facts. According to epistemological disjunctivism the connection is very direct indeed, since being in possession of the relevant epistemic support actually entails that the proposition believed is true.

Many, if not most, in epistemology take it as a given that such a combination of theses is simply incoherent. If that's right, then, *a fortiori*, epistemological disjunctivism cannot offer a way through the epistemic externalism/internalism *impasse*. According to most epistemologists, that is, we need to choose between two options on this score. On the one hand, if our beliefs enjoy an adequate epistemic support in virtue of the relevant worldly facts obtaining, then there will inevitably be a significant degree of reflective opacity in the epistemic standing of our beliefs and hence epistemic responsibility will be undermined. On the other hand, if the epistemic standing of our beliefs is to a large extent a function of factors which are reflectively accessible to us, then there will be a significant degree of reflective transparency in the epistemic standing of our beliefs (enough to enable us to be epistemically responsible for them), but at the cost of allowing our epistemic standings to potentially 'cut free' from the relevant worldly facts altogether. Such a conception of the epistemic externalism/internalism distinction clearly leaves no space at all for epistemological disjunctivism.

But suppose for a moment that the epistemological disjunctivist view was available. Wouldn't that change our epistemological theorising beyond recognition? In terms of the epistemic externalism/internalism debate the positive ramifications are clear. For we would now be in a position to, as it were, have our cake and eat it too. On the one hand, we have the connection to the worldly facts that is so attractive about the epistemic externalist position. On the other hand, we have the reflective access to the factors relevant to our epistemic standings such that we can retain the appeal of epistemic internalism when it comes to the issue of epistemic responsibility. In short, we can have reflective transparency in our epistemic standings without paying the price of losing the essential connection between our epistemic standings and the relevant worldly facts.

The attractions of epistemological disjunctivism do not end there. Think, for example, of the theoretical options that would suddenly become available as regards such perennial epistemological issues as the problem of radical scepticism. In this debate we see a version of the dilemma regarding the epistemic externalism/internalism distinction that we just set out gaining an analogous deleterious purchase on our thinking. Opting for the epistemic internalist way with the sceptic seems to involve a kind of radical retreat from the world, such that the epistemic standing of our beliefs, while immune from sceptical attack, is only so immune because this epistemic standing is independent of the relevant worldly facts in the first place. This 'victory' over the sceptic is clearly Pyrrhic (if you'll excuse the pun). But opting for epistemic externalism as a route out of the sceptical predicament seems no better on this score, for it appears to side-step the issue altogether by making our epistemic standings conditional on the obtaining of worldly facts which one lacks any reflective access to and which are in any case in dispute in a debate with the sceptic. In contrast, if epistemological disjunctivism were a viable theory then a potential route out of this problem becomes available, since we can now appeal to reflectively accessible elements of our epistemic standings which entail facts about the world. Thus, the problem is not side-stepped by appealing to facts beyond our reflective ken, nor is a tactical retreat necessary when what we have reflective access to can be factive in this fashion.

It is for these reasons that I refer to epistemological disjunctivism as the 'holy grail' of epistemology. On the one hand, its theoretical benefits are potentially enormous. On the other hand, there is something mysterious—bordering on the magical—about the view that makes it seem just too good to be true. For how can the epistemic support for one's perceptual belief be both factive *and* reflectively accessible? *Prima facie*, this just doesn't seem at all possible.

Here is my strategy. My primary objective is to set out what epistemological disjunctivism amounts to and to show that this proposal is not in fact subject to the kind of problems that one might be initially inclined to pose for it. In this way, I hope to demonstrate that contemporary epistemology has been far too premature in dismissing this theoretical option *tout court*, even despite its clear *prima facie* implausibility. If I can achieve even this much with this text, then this would be significant progress, since this would entail that contemporary epistemology has an obligation to examine the view afresh and reconsider just what might be wrong about it. I also have a secondary objective, however, which is to set out in outline what implications such a position might have for standard epistemological debates, such as the problem of radical scepticism. This will hopefully have the effect of indicating what attractions the view can hold while also, along the way, offering more detail about what the proposal involves.

This strategy is reflected in the way this book has been composed. Rather than opting for a chapter-by-chapter structure, I've instead split the text into three parts which feature an extended essay on a specific area of relevance. Part one aims to set out the epistemological disjunctivist position in outline and to delineate the three main *prima facie* problems that afflict this view. As part of a general exploration of the view some of the motivations for the position are considered along with its relationship to metaphysical forms of disjunctivism. A novel construal of the relationship between seeing that *p* and knowing that *p* is then put forward, and it is also shown in some detail how epistemological disjunctivism challenges the conventional understanding of the epistemic externalism/internalism distinction. In light of this exploration of the proposal, a solution to two of the three *prima facie* problems (the *access problem* and the *basis problem*) is offered, but the remaining problem (the *distinguishability problem*) is left for part two.

Part two aims to provide the wider epistemological structure required to make sense of epistemological disjunctivism such that it can avoid the remaining *prima facie* problem put forward in part one. In particular, a distinction between favouring and discriminating epistemic support is argued for, a distinction which it is claimed all epistemological proposals should endorse, regardless of whether they are independently committed to epistemological disjunctivism. This distinction has a number of important ramifications for contemporary epistemology, and it is shown that it lends support to a particular kind of relevant alternatives account of perceptual knowledge. Crucially, however, it is also argued that this distinction offers particular assistance to epistemological disjunctivism by enabling it to evade the remaining *prima facie* problem delineated in part one. By the end of part two the proposal has thus been quite extensively explored and it has been shown that far from being a hopeless view it is in fact not susceptible to the *prima facie* problems that have been levelled at it after all. In short, a case has been made for treating epistemological disjunctivism as a live option.

Part three builds on the work done in parts one and two to further motivate the proposal by showing how it can offer a new way of dealing with the problem of radical scepticism. This is done by locating the position relative to the Moorean-style responses to radical scepticism that have recently been offered in the literature and showing how epistemological disjunctivism results in a distinctive version of neo-Mooreanism. In particular, it is argued that whilst standard neo-Moorean proposals are usually cast along traditional epistemic internalist or externalist lines, and so face the usual difficulties that afflict responses to radical scepticism of this sort, a variety of neo-Mooreanism which is cast along epistemological disjunctivist lines offers a very different way of dealing with the problem, one that has some key advantages. In order for this anti-sceptical proposal to be plausible, however, it is essential that an explanation is offered of why the relevant Moorean anti-sceptical assertions seem so inappropriate, since on this view it is far from obvious why they should be. Accordingly, an account of their impropriety is put forward. As part of the wider discussion of the nature of this anti-sceptical proposal part three also explores such issues as the dialectical commitments in play in the debate with the sceptic, and the relevance of John McDowell's writings on this topic.

One final point about this work is in order. The reader should note that my concerns here, while in one sense quite radical—in that I am trying to motivate a position that has dramatic implications for epistemology, and which most think is simply unavailable—are also in another sense quite restricted. My aim is to set out an interesting and thought-provoking view within a relatively short book. There is another book that one could write on this topic, one that drew out all the relevant connections between epistemological disjunctivism and disjunctivism more generally, which applied such a view to all species of knowledge and not just perceptual knowledge, and which developed in complete detail the epistemological disjunctivist position and its implications for contemporary epistemology. Such a book would undoubtedly be an interesting contribution to contemporary epistemological debate, but it would also be a mammoth undertaking. Worse, I fear that such a book would not be widely read, for given the in-built resistance to epistemological disjunctivism within current thinking in epistemology it would be very unlikely that many would trouble themselves to read such an ambitious tome. With that in mind, it seems to me to be far better to write a shorter book which can reach out to the main current of debate within epistemology, with a view to facilitating a constructive engagement between epistemological disjunctivism and alternative, and more mainstream, positions.

There are two quite specific issues that I won't be addressing in depth here and which deserve mention. The first is that I don't discuss in any great detail how epistemological disjunctivism relates to the more commonly discussed *metaphysical* disjunctivism, except to mark the contrast early on. As I explain in part one, I hold that we can reasonably treat epistemological disjunctivism as being logically independent from metaphysical disjunctivism (at least to the extent that a commitment to the former does not necessitate a commitment to the latter), but in any case it would take me too far afield to offer an extended discussion of this contrast, interesting though it is.

The second issue is the relationship between the epistemological disjunctivist view that I set out here and the position in the literature that it mostly closely resembles, due to McDowell.[4] There can be no doubt that McDowell is the foremost exponent of a proposal of this general sort, though his view is often misinterpreted and misunderstood. It is also certainly the case that my own thinking on this topic directly emerges out of reading and engaging with McDowell's work. That said, however, I do not wish this text to be saddled with the additional burden of being the mouthpiece for a McDowellian epistemology. Partly, this is because there is very little consensus regarding what McDowell's view in this regard actually is.[5] Partly, this is because the view I defend here, while *inspired* by McDowell's writings, is not meant to be in any way a rendering of his view. (My mistakes are, therefore, completely my own.) And partly this is because there is, I suggest, such a wholesale misunderstanding of McDowell's position in the contemporary literature that it would be a very long book indeed which attempted to unravel the genuine from the perceived article. Thus, although I will in places discuss McDowell's writings on this topic (particularly in part three), for the most part I will be setting aside the question of how epistemological disjunctivism as I characterize it here conforms to or departs from the kind of view that McDowell defends.

In any case, if I can motivate epistemological disjunctivism then these lacunas will be small beer, so let us now turn to the task in hand.

Notes to Introduction

1. When I first used this description in a public arena, as part of a talk I gave at a conference on *Disjunctivism* at the University of Glasgow in June 2005, I wasn't aware of anyone else employing this terminology. At this conference, however, there was another talk, by Alex Byrne and Heather Logue, which also used this description to describe a roughly similar view. (The papers from the Glasgow conference were ultimately published as Haddock and Macpherson (2008*a*). See, in particular, Pritchard (2008*b*) and Byrne and Logue (2008).) Since then I've seen this terminology used a number of times, most recently in Soteriou (2009), Brogaard (2010), and Madison (2010). Note that in what follows 'epistemological disjunctivism' refers specifically to the view as I present it and not to other positions which may fall under this heading.

2. Of course, there are so-called 'hybrid' accounts on offer in the literature, but such views are not (usually at any rate) meant to be challenges to the idea that the epistemic externalism/internalism distinction is exclusive and exhaustive. Rather, these proposals are meant to be closer to the centre ground than other positions in the literature, such that while they are better able to accommodate insights from both sides of the distinction they are still meant to ultimately fall on one of the sides of the distinction. (In this regard, consider, for example, the 'hybrid' version of epistemic internalism offered by Alston (1988).)

3. Indeed, that epistemic internalism has this consequence is often held to be an *advantage* of the view relative to epistemic externalism, even though it is an advantage which clearly in other respects puts the position at a disadvantage. The intuition in play here is often labelled the 'new evil genius' intuition—see especially Lehrer and Cohen (1983)—and it will be explored in more detail in part one.

4. For his clearest endorsement of the view, see McDowell (1995), although he does not express the view in anything like the direct fashion put forward here. In this work he argues that one's empirical reason for believing a certain external world proposition, *p*, can be that one *sees that p* is the case where *seeing that p* is factive. He also maintains that such factive reasons can be nevertheless reflectively accessible to the agent—indeed, he demands (though not in quite these words) that they be accessible for they must be able to serve as the agent's reasons. For example, in criticizing what he calls the 'hybrid conception of knowledge' (on which one's rational support for one's perceptual beliefs is never factive), McDowell writes:

> In the hybrid conception, a satisfactory standing in the space of reasons is only part of what knowledge is; truth is an extra requirement. So two subjects can be alike in respect of the satisfactoriness of their standing in the space of reasons, although only one of them is a knower, because only in her case is what she takes to be so actually so. But if its being so is

external to her operations in the space of reasons, how can it not be outside the reach of her rational powers? And if it is outside the reach of her rational powers, how can its being so be the crucial element in an intelligible conception of her knowing that it is so—what makes the relevant difference between her and the other subject? Its being so is conceived as external to the only thing that is supposed to be epistemologically significant about the knower herself, her satisfactory standing in the space of reasons. (McDowell 1995, 884)

This passage requires some interpretation. First, I interpret the expression 'outside the reach of [*an agent's*] rational powers' in such a way that, for some fact *p* to be 'outside the reach of [*an agent's*] rational powers' is for *p* to be unable to serve as an agent's reason for belief. Second, there is a question about why McDowell takes it to follow from *p*'s not being able to serve as an agent's reason for belief that it cannot be an epistemologically significant feature of the agent herself. I suggest that McDowell is willing to make this inference because he holds the following view: for *p* to be able to serve as an agent's reason for belief, the agent must be able to know that *p*, and know it by reflection alone. Furthermore—I take McDowell to hold—only what the agent can know by reflection alone can be an epistemologically significant feature of the agent herself. Here is some textual support for the latter attribution to McDowell:

I agree with [Elizabeth Fricker] that we lose the point of invoking the space of reasons if we allow someone to possess a justification even if it is outside his reflective reach. (McDowell 1994, 199)

Since McDowell does invoke the space of reasons, he must think that there is some point to doing so, and so he must think that someone cannot possess a justification that is 'outside his reflective reach'. Furthermore, I assume that for something to be 'outside [*the agent's*] reflective reach', in McDowell's terms, is for the agent not to be able to know it by reflection alone. So the agent's justification—the rational support she possesses for her belief—must be such that she can know it by reflection alone. See also the following passage:

[O]ne's epistemic standing on some question cannot be intelligibly constituted, even in part, by matters blankly external to how it is with one subjectively. For how could such matters be other than beyond one's ken? And how could matters beyond one's ken make any difference to one's epistemic standing. (McDowell 1982, 26)

As I am reading McDowell, the demand in play here is precisely that one's rational support for one's beliefs had better be subjectively available in the sense of being reflectively accessible (i.e., within one's reflective 'ken').

The reader might also find it useful to consult McDowell's 2011 Aquinas lecture (see McDowell 2011). Although this is largely focused on Burge's account of perceptual entitlement—in particular, as it is expressed in Burge (2003)—McDowell does also relate his discussion to wider themes in epistemology. For a useful discussion of this work, see Black (2011).

5. To be fair to his commentators, McDowell is himself to some degree culpable in this regard since he does have a rather enigmatic writing style. As one prominent commentator famously put it: 'McDowell is a strong swimmer, but his stroke is not to be emulated' (Wright 1996, 252).

PART ONE

Epistemological Disjunctivism in Outline

§1. Epistemological Disjunctivism: A First Pass

Let us be bold and dive right into a discussion of the core thesis of the view that interests us and proceed from there:

Epistemological Disjunctivism: The Core Thesis
In paradigmatic cases of perceptual knowledge an agent, *S*, has perceptual knowledge that ϕ in virtue of being in possession of rational support, *R*, for her belief that ϕ which is both *factive* (i.e., *R*'s obtaining entails ϕ) and *reflectively accessible* to *S*.

A few observations are in order. First, notice that the kind of knowledge we are focusing on here is quite restricted. In particular, we are specifically talking about *perceptual* knowledge.[1] It may well be possible to offer a variant of epistemological disjunctivism which is applicable to knowledge in general, but it will greatly assist our discussion to consider the proposal with the focus narrowed. If epistemological disjunctivism has application anywhere, then it will be here, and it will be news enough if the view applies to this species of knowledge. In addition, the core epistemological disjunctivist thesis only concerns *paradigm* cases of perceptual knowledge, and thus it is a further question what implications this view has for non-paradigmatic cases of perceptual knowledge (I clarify below what is meant by 'paradigm' in this context). As we will see, this limited claim is controversial enough to warrant our attention.

Second, notice that the epistemic support that interests us is rational in nature. This epistemic support has some distinctive properties, however. On the one hand, it is reflectively accessible to the subject, where this usually means that the subject can come to know through reflection alone that she is in possession of this rational support. That the rational support for one's believing that *p* must be reflectively accessible in this way is not usually thought controversial, and it is easy to see why.[2] For if this rational support were not so accessible—if, in particular, it was opaque to one that one's belief enjoyed this rational support—then it would be hard to see why it would count as rationally supporting your belief that *p*. Where the epistemological disjunctivist parts company with standard views, however, is with regard to the claim that this rational support can be *factive*, such that its obtaining entails the target proposition. That is, one's rational support for one's belief that *p* can be both reflectively accessible and such that its obtaining entails *p*, even when (as in the cases that interest us) *p* is an empirical proposition.

The particular kind of rational support that the epistemological disjunctivist claims that our beliefs enjoy in paradigm cases of perceptual knowledge is that provided by *seeing that* the target proposition obtains. So when one has paradigmatic perceptual knowledge of a proposition, *p*, one's reflectively accessible rational support for believing that *p* is that one *sees that p*. Seeing that *p* is factive, however, in that if it is the case that one sees that *p* then *p* must be true. Paradigmatic perceptual knowledge is thus held by epistemological disjunctivism to be supported by a rational basis which is both reflectively accessible and factive (even though the known proposition is empirical).

That the perceptual knowledge in question enjoys such factive rational support does not of course preclude it from enjoying other forms of epistemic support as well, whether rational support of a different non-factive type or non-rational support. For example, given that the agent genuinely has knowledge, then the target belief will almost certainly as a matter of fact be reliably formed, and most epistemologists would grant that this provides some non-rational epistemic support for that belief (though it is of course controversial just what role this type of epistemic support should play in one's theory of knowledge). Crucially, however, the claim is that paradigm cases of perceptual knowledge always involve the specific kind of factive rational support just outlined, where this rational support is *sufficient* for knowledge of the target proposition. Thus although the belief in these cases might inevitably enjoy other forms of epistemic support (e.g., by being reliably formed), these other forms of epistemic support are not necessary for this belief to count as knowledge. Note too that this claim is also consistent with the idea that non-paradigmatic cases of perceptual knowledge might be acquired in such a way that the agent lacks any kind of rational support for her beliefs (*a fortiori*, it is also consistent with the idea that non-paradigmatic perceptual knowledge might be gained in such a way that the agent lacks factive rational support for her beliefs).

The disjunctivist aspect of the view is brought out by considering how the rational support one has for one's beliefs radically differs in the following pair of cases. On the one hand, we have a 'good' case where the agent possesses (paradigmatic) perceptual knowledge. On the other hand, we have a corresponding 'bad' case where the agent's experiences are introspectively indistinguishable in which she lacks perceptual knowledge of the target proposition but nonetheless blamelessly supposes that she possesses such knowledge.[3] A standard view about reflectively accessible rational support is that the agents in these pairs of good and bad cases possess the same degree of reflectively accessible rational support for their beliefs (we will explore the motivation for this claim below).[4] The epistemological disjunctivist rejects this picture and holds instead that the rational support reflectively accessible to the agents in these pairs of cases is in fact radically different. In the good case the agent possesses paradigmatic perceptual knowledge and so is in possession of rational support which is both reflectively accessible and factive. In the bad case, in contrast, she lacks such knowledge and hence lacks this type of rational support too (we will consider what, if any, rational support is available to the subject in the bad case below).

As an illustration, consider the following pair of cases. In the first case, the agent genuinely perceives that there is a tree before her in epistemically excellent conditions (there is no deception in play in the environment, her faculties are working normally, and so on). On the basis of this perception she forms the belief that there is a tree before her. In the second case, the agent is in a situation which is experientially introspectively indistinguishable from the first, and hence which blamelessly prompts her to form a belief in the same proposition with as much conviction as in the first case. Crucially, however, her belief is formed in highly sub-optimal conditions. To make the contrast particularly clear (we will be considering a continuum of pairs of cases of this sort below), let us suppose that our agent in this second case is simply hallucinating that there is a tree before her and in fact is being visually presented with no specific object at all.

As we will see below, on standard views of reflectively accessible rational support, the rational support that is reflectively accessible to the agents in these two cases is the same. According to epistemological disjunctivism, in contrast, the rational support reflectively accessible to the agents in these two cases is very different. In particular, in the first case the agent's reflectively accessible rational support will be the factive ground that she sees that there is a tree before her, and she will have perceptual knowledge that there is a tree before her in virtue of possessing this rational basis for her belief. But whatever the nature of the reflectively accessible rational support in the second case—and one possibility here, as we will see below, is that the agent possesses *no* rational support—it cannot be of this factive sort (aside from anything else, the target proposition is false in the second case). Moreover, notice that however we understand the rational support in the second case, it is not merely a 'stunted' version of the rational support in the first case, as if the latter were just the former supplemented in some way with additional rational support. Rather, the two rational standings are radically different *in kind* (this is what makes this epistemological proposal *disjunctivist*).

§2. Motivating Epistemological Disjunctivism

Even those radically opposed to epistemological disjunctivism will likely grant that the view accords with a commonsense way of thinking, and talking, about perceptual reasons. That is, in response to a challenge to a claim to (perceptually) know I might well respond by citing a factive perceptual reason in defence of my claim, which suggests that we do, ordinarily at least, allow factive reasons to offer sufficient rational support for our perceptual knowledge.

For example, suppose I tell my line manager over the phone that my colleague is at work today (thereby representing myself as perceptually knowing this to be the case), and she expresses scepticism about this (perhaps because she falsely believes that my colleague always skips work when she isn't there). In response I might naturally say that I know that she's at work today because I can see that she's in work—she's standing right in front of me.

The naturalness of this conversational exchange implies that it is the epistemological disjunctivist who is working with the commonsense position, and her detractor who is offering the revisionistic view.[5] Of course, this fact in itself may mean very little when set against the grander theoretical scheme, since sometimes our commonsense convictions are plainly wrong, and it is in any case notoriously hard to read our commonsense convictions off everyday language use in this way. Perhaps, for example, we only cite factive reasons in the manner just described because we are implicitly bracketing the kind of error-possibilities which could count against the reason being factive. If that's right, then the citing of a factive reason has a kind of elliptical form, in that it is only given that certain shared presuppositions of the conversational context are in play that it is legitimate to cite the factive reason in support of one's challenged claim to know. So, for example, it is only because a wide range of error-possibilities are implicitly being set aside that it is legitimate for me to reply to the challenge to my claim to know that my colleague is at work by citing the factive reason that I can see that she is at work. This description of events would, however, provide little support for epistemological disjunctivism, since it would leave it an open question whether the factive reason in play can ever be sufficient for perceptual knowledge of the target proposition.[6]

The importance of the appeal to commonsense lies in the fact that if one is able to dress one's position up in the garments of commonsense, then this gives one's view a default status relative to opposing views which revise our commonsense convictions. Of course, as just noted, such a default status is highly defeasible, in that it can be undermined by wider theoretical considerations. Nonetheless, it is important to a thesis like epistemological disjunctivism that it is able to appeal to this default status since it is a position which is standardly represented by the prevailing conventional wisdom in epistemology as the revisionary option. If the epistemological disjunctivist is right that we often speak in a way that would support this view, however, then this goes a long way towards levelling the dialectical playing field in this regard.

In practice, the reason why epistemological disjunctivism is not widely adopted is because it is held to face several fatal theoretical problems. Accordingly, whatever commonsense support it might have, it is thought to be a complete non-starter as a theoretical position. We will consider some of these problems in a moment. The overarching strategy in this book is to try to show that in fact epistemological disjunctivism doesn't face any obvious fatal theoretical problems at all, and thus that it should be treated as a viable theoretical position. Moreover, the further aim is to demonstrate that if epistemological disjunctivism were true, then it would be a tremendously powerful position, one that offers compelling responses to important episte-mological problems, such as the problem of radical scepticism. If one could in addition show that it occupied a default position in our thinking about perceptual knowledge, then that would be the icing on the cake.

In a nutshell, then, I shall be motivating epistemological disjunctivism by showing that this is an attractive position which we would want to hold *if* it were theoretically available, and further showing that it *is* theoretically available, contrary to the prevailing conventional wisdom in epistemology.

§3. Three *Prima Facie* Problems for Epistemological Disjunctivism

Epistemological disjunctivism poses a radical challenge to a standard view about the nature of reflectively accessible rational support. In doing so, it occupies a region of logical space in epistemology that many hold is simply unavailable. In particular, what is puzzling (and, many would claim, simply incoherent) about the epistemological disjunctivist proposal is the idea that one's rational support for one's (paradigmatic) perceptual knowledge could be both reflectively accessible and factive. We can delineate three interrelated *prima facie* worries here.

The first, and perhaps most immediate, is the concern that such a view will directly generate a kind of 'McKinsey-style' problem—i.e., a problem of a parallel sort to that which is widely alleged to face the combination of first-person authority and content externalism.[7] In essence, this problem concerns the fact that according to (some famous versions of) content externalism a prerequisite of one's beliefs having a particular content can be that a certain specific worldly fact (or facts) obtain. Given that content externalism is a philosophical thesis, it seems that it can be known a priori. But given first-person authority, that one has a belief with a certain content is also something that is plausibly in the market for reflective (and thus non-empirical/a priori) knowledge. Thus it seems that if both first-person authority and content externalism are true, then one ought to be able to come to know specific facts about one's environment simply through reflection, and for most this would be a *reductio* of this conjunction of theses.

The parallel problem that faces epistemological disjunctivism concerns the fact that one can surely know a priori that seeing that p entails p. Thus, if one can come to know by reflection alone that one's rational support for one's belief that p—where p is a specific proposition about one's environment—is that one sees that p, then surely one can through further a priori reflection come to know p itself. But, as with the McKinsey problem that faces the combination of content externalism and first-person authority, it seems incredible that one could come to know a specific fact about one's environment purely through reflection.

In order to illustrate this problem, consider a concrete case. Suppose one believes that John is at home, and that one's reflectively accessible rational support for this belief is that one sees that John is at home (i.e., this is a case of paradigmatic perceptual knowledge, as the epistemological disjunctivist describes it). Given that one also (we might assume) knows a priori that seeing that p entails p, it seems that one can further conclude, purely by undertaking a competent deduction (and hence by reflection alone), that John is at home. But now it seems that one is coming to know a specific empirical fact about one's environment purely by a reflective and thus non-empirical process, and that sounds absurd. Call this the *access problem* for epistemological disjunctivism.

The second problem facing epistemological disjunctivism is closely related to the first, and concerns the fact that if one does have reflective access to factive reasons in cases involving paradigmatic perceptual knowledge, then it is hard to see how one can reconcile this claim with the undeniable truth that there are parallel introspectively indistinguishable scenarios in which one lacks a factive reason but where, nonetheless, one continues to blamelessly suppose that one possesses it. So, for example, let us grant that it is indeed presently true that I see that there is a computer in front of me and that I have paradigmatic perceptual knowledge of this proposition on this basis. We will discuss further below what seeing that p involves, but whatever it involves we can imagine a parallel case which is experientially introspectively indistinguishable from the case just described in which I don't see that there is a computer before me because it simply isn't true that there is a computer before me. Suppose, for example, that I am the victim of some sort of trick of the light which makes it look to all intents and purposes as if there is computer in front of me when in fact I am looking at an empty desk. In the deceived case I will blamelessly think that I see that there is a computer before me, when in fact this is not the case.

Here is the problem. If, in the non-deceived case, one has reflective access to the relevant factive reason as epistemological disjunctivism maintains, then why doesn't it follow that one can introspectively distinguish between the non-deceived and deceived cases after all, contrary to intuition? For in the non-deceived case there *is* something reflectively accessible to one which is not reflectively accessible in the deceived case—*viz.*, the target factive reason. Accordingly, it seems that by epistemological disjunctivist lights it should be very easy to introspectively distinguish between the deceived and the non-deceived cases, since all one needs to do is see if the relevant factive reason is reflectively available. In short, the problem is that it is difficult to see how epistemological disjunctivism can square its claim that the reflectively accessible reasons in support of one's perceptual knowledge can nonetheless be factive with the undeniable truth that there can be pairs of cases like that just described which are introspectively indistinguishable. Call this the *distinguishability problem* for epistemological disjunctivism.

The third problem concerns the very idea of a factive reason providing epistemic support for knowledge. On most views, after all, seeing that *p* just is a way of knowing that *p* (i.e., it is knowing that *p* via visual perception).[8] This *seems* right. We've already noted that seeing that *p*, like knowing that *p*, is factive. Moreover, it is also true that seeing that *p*, like knowing that *p*, expresses a rather robust epistemic relation that one bears to *p*. For example, the agent who thinks that he can see a computer before him, but who is forming this belief in epistemically poor conditions (perhaps because he is presently dazed after a bump on the head), does not intuitively count as seeing that there is a computer before him, even if he is indeed presently faced with a computer. A natural explanation for this is that his visual perception of the computer, while veridical, does not put him in a position to know the target proposition, and this reinforces the idea that seeing that *p* is just a way of knowing that *p*.

The problem, however, is that if this is indeed the right way to think about the relationship between seeing that *p* and knowing that *p*, then it is hard to understand how seeing that *p* could constitute one's epistemic *basis* for knowing that *p*. After all, on this view seeing that *p* already presupposes knowledge that *p* on account of how it is just a way of knowing that *p*. But how then could seeing that *p* constitute one's epistemic basis for knowing that *p*? Call this the *basis problem* for epistemological disjunctivism.

All three problems will require an answer if epistemological disjuncti-vism is to have any plausibility, but for now I ask the reader to set these concerns to one side so that we can explore the view in more detail. As we will see, getting clear on what the view involves will be key to under-standing how it can deal with these problems.

§4. Metaphysical and Epistemological Disjunctivism

It will be useful at this juncture to examine how epistemological disjunctivism relates to other disjunctivist positions in the literature, particularly those which might be more familiar to the reader. In particular, it is important to distinguish epistemological disjunctivism from the kind of *metaphysical* disjunctivism that has been widely discussed with regard to the philosophy of perceptual experience.[9]

Although there is a range of metaphysical disjunctivist views,[10] what they have in common is a rejection of the idea that the nature of one's perceptual experience is the same regardless of whether one is having a normal veridical perceptual experience as opposed to being the victim of an introspectively indistinguishable experience which is in fact an illusion (roughly, where a different object is presented to one) or an hallucination (roughly, where no object is presented to one). On a standard (non-disjunctivist) view about perceptual experiences, where they are indistinguishable in this way then they are essentially the same experiences. At the very least, they have a shared essential nature. In contrast, metaphysical disjunctivists hold that veridical perceptual experiences are not essentially the same as the experiences involved in corresponding cases involving illusion and (especially) hallucination. More specifically, these experiences do not have a shared essential nature.[11]

From this basic starting-point, a range of potential versions of metaphysical disjunctivism can be delineated.[12] What is of particular interest for our purposes, however, is the general way in which metaphysical disjunctivism relates to epistemological disjunctivism. In particular, we need to determine whether epistemological disjunctivism entails (a version of) metaphysical disjunctivism, since if it does then the correctness of the former is hostage to the correctness of the latter.

It is reasonably clear that epistemological disjunctivism does not in itself entail metaphysical disjunctivism. For that the rational standing available to the agent in normal veridical perceptual experiences and corresponding (introspectively indistinguishable) cases of illusion and hallucination are radically different does not in itself entail that there is no common metaphysical essence to the experiences of the agent in both cases. Perhaps there is a common metaphysical essence to the perceptual experiences in these cases, but that it has no direct bearing on the rational support available to the agent in support of the target perceptual beliefs. If that's right, then in defending epistemological disjunctivism one is not thereby committed to defending metaphysical disjunctivism as well. Instead, one would need to defend further claims in order to supply the relevant 'bridge' between these two theses.[13,14]

Of course, even though epistemological disjunctivism might not entail metaphysical disjunctivism, it could be nonetheless dialectically affiliated. In particular, it could be that it is hard to motivate the epistemological disjunctivist position without appeal to a form of metaphysical disjunctivism. This claim certainly does have bite. After all, one might naturally claim that if there is such a radical difference between the reflectively accessible rational support that one possesses in the relevant pairs of cases as the epistemological disjunctivist claims, then that will naturally incline one towards endorsing a disjunctivist view of the metaphysics of perceptual experience. In a nutshell, the disjunctivist view of the metaphysics of perceptual experience seems to offer the most natural way of explaining why there is this radical epistemic difference in these pairs of cases—*viz.*, the reflectively accessible rational support is different because the very nature of one's experiences is different.

Even so, the critical point is that one does not automatically become committed to metaphysical disjunctivism in virtue of endorsing epistemological disjunctivism, and so we can leave it as an open question for our purposes whether the epistemological disjunctivist should also be a metaphysical disjunctivist. With this point in mind, in what follows we will focus our attentions solely on epistemological disjunctivism and set to one side how this view interacts with related views about the metaphysics of perceptual experience. In doing so, we will enable a far greater focus on the epistemological issues associated with epistemological disjunctivism.

§5. Seeing That *P* and Knowing That *P*

As noted above, the standard view about the relationship between seeing that *p* and knowing that *p* is that the former is simply a more specific version of the latter, such that seeing that *p* is just a particular way of knowing that *p*. One consequence of this view is that if one sees that *p* then one knows that *p*. Call this the *entailment thesis*.[15] We also noted above that there is a strong *prima facie* case for the entailment thesis in that seeing that *p*, like knowing that *p*, is both factive and robustly epistemic. It is, however, the entailment thesis which generates the basis problem considered above, since if seeing that *p* entails knowing that *p*, then it is hard to see how it can be part of the rational basis for one's paradigmatic perceptual knowledge as epistemological disjunctivism maintains.

I will be arguing that epistemological disjunctivism can evade the basis problem by resisting the conventional wisdom embodied by the entailment thesis. In particular, I will be maintaining that one can capture the close connections between seeing that *p* and knowing that *p* without having to endorse the entailment thesis. I will then further motivate the alternative view that I propose by showing how we can embed this view within a more sophisticated account of 'good' and 'bad' cases than that which is suggested by the entailment thesis. It is thus shown how rejecting the entailment thesis is a viable theoretical option for the proponent of epistemological disjunctivism. Hence, insofar as epistemological disjunctivism really does have the extensive theoretical advantages that I claim it has, then there is a solid theoretical basis, all things considered, to reject the entailment thesis and endorse in its place the alternative account of the relationship between seeing that *p* and knowing that *p* that I offer.

Key to any plausible rejection of the entailment thesis will be finding a way to accommodate the insight which motivates the entailment thesis—*viz.*, that seeing that *p*, like knowing that *p*, is both factive and robustly epistemic. To this end, a crucial distinction that we need to draw is between being in a state that guarantees knowledge and being in a state that *guarantees that one is in a good position* to gain knowledge, even if one is unable to properly exploit this opportunity. I want to suggest that seeing that *p* is factive and robustly epistemic in the weaker latter sense rather than in the more robust former sense. That is, seeing that *p* and knowing that *p* come apart—such that the former can properly be thought of as providing an epistemic basis for the latter—and come apart in just those cases in which an agent, on account of seeing that *p*, is thereby in a good position to gain knowledge that *p* and yet is unable to properly exploit this opportunity.

One important contrast between seeing that *p* and knowing that *p* is that the latter, but not the former, entails belief in *p*.[16] Suppose, for example, that one is in a situation in which one is genuinely visually presented with a barn and circumstances are in fact epistemically good (there's no deception in play, one's faculties are functioning correctly, and so on). But now suppose further that one has been told, by an otherwise reliable informant, that one is presently being deceived (that one is in barn façade county, say), even though this is in fact not the case. Clearly, in such a case one ought not to believe the target proposition, and hence one cannot possibly know this proposition either. (Indeed, if one did continue to believe the target proposition even despite the presence of this undefeated defeater, then one would still lack knowledge.) Does it follow that one does not see that the target proposition obtains? I suggest not.

It is certainly true that one sees a barn in this case, since one surely stands in the right kind of relationship to the barn to ensure this much. But of course that doesn't settle the issue that concerns us, which is whether one *sees that* there is a barn before one, which is undoubtedly a more (epistemically) demanding relation to be in. Here's a reason for thinking that one does indeed stand in this relation in this case, despite one's lack of knowledge (and possible lack of belief also). For suppose that one were to discover subsequently that the testimony one received was false, but that everything else one knows about the circumstances in which one was presented with this (apparent) barn remained the same. Wouldn't one now retrospectively treat oneself as having earlier *seen that* there was a barn? Think, for example, about how one would describe one's situation in this regard were one to be asked about it. Wouldn't it be most natural to say that one did see that there was a barn in the field, rather than to 'hedge' one's assertion by saying, for example, that one merely thought that one saw a barn?

But if that's right, then it does appear that there is good reason for supposing that one does see that there is a barn in this case, even though one can't know the target proposition, and even though one ought not to even believe this proposition (and most probably won't believe it). Moreover, this way of thinking about this case highlights the importance of the distinction between being in a state that guarantees knowledge and being in a state that guarantees that one is in a good position to gain knowledge. For given that the defeater in play is misleading, one is *in fact* in a good position to gain knowledge of the target proposition in this case, it is just that one's inability to defeat the misleading defeater undermines one's ability to exploit this epistemic opportunity.[17,18] (This is a point that we will return to presently.)

Interestingly, this point about the entailment thesis with regard to seeing that *p* and knowing that *p* generalizes to other factive states which are also often thought to stand in an entailment relation to knowing that *p*. For example, consider the factive state of *remembering that p*. Like seeing that *p*, remembering that *p* is factive. If you really are remembering that *p*—as opposed to merely thinking that you are remembering that *p*—then *p* must be the case. And like seeing that *p*, remembering that *p* is also robustly epistemic. Merely thinking that you are remembering that *p* and *p* being the case won't suffice for genuinely remembering that *p*. Instead, you need to stand in the kind of epistemic relationships to *p* that are characteristic of knowing that *p*. Unsurprisingly, then, many claim that remembering that *p* entails knowing that *p*, just like seeing that *p*.[19]

But with our distinction between being in a state that guarantees knowledge and merely being in a state that *guarantees that one is in a good position* to gain knowledge, we should be suspicious of this line of thinking. Indeed, consider a parallel case to that which we just considered regarding seeing that *p*, where an agent is in an otherwise excellent epistemic position except that they are presented with a misleading defeater. Imagine, for example, that one is in a state such that one would have otherwise quite rightly taken oneself to be remembering that *p*, but that one doesn't form this judgement because one is presented with a defeater (e.g., a good undefeated ground for thinking that not-*p*). But suppose that it subsequently comes to light that this defeater is in fact a misleading defeater, and thus that there was no epistemic bar to one forming the relevant judgement after all.

Here is the crux. Once apprised of these facts, wouldn't one now describe one's previous state as being one of remembering that p after all? Crucially, however, one surely would not describe one's previous state as being one of knowing that p, given the presence of the undefeated misleading defeater (and given also the related fact that one did not even believe that p at the time). But if that's right, then the chain of reasoning in play earlier with regard to the entailment thesis from seeing that p to knowing that p also undermines a parallel entailment thesis from remembering that p to knowing that p. (Indeed, I suspect it undermines several such entailment theses involving other factive states and knowing that p, though this is not the place to explore this further.)

In any case, back to seeing that p and knowing that p. The important point for our purposes is that with the entailment thesis rejected the basis problem is blocked, and hence a core difficulty facing epistemological disjunctivism is dealt with.[20] There is still more to be said on this score, however, since the rejection of the entailment thesis behoves us to look again at how we are thinking of good and bad cases, and how, in particular, such cases relate to seeing that p and knowing that p.

With the entailment thesis in play, there is a very straightforward way of drawing a contrast between pairs of 'good' and 'bad' cases of perception (i.e., cases which are introspectively indistinguishable and yet which elicit very different epistemic responses). That is, the good case will be an epistemically propitious scenario in which the agent sees that p, and hence also knows that p via perception. In contrast, the bad case will be a scenario which is epistemically deficient in some significant way, such that the agent doesn't see that p, and hence doesn't (on this rational basis anyway) perceptually know that p either.

This simple picture gains support from a certain range of cases that we might consider. Imagine, for example, a good case in which the agent genuinely sees a barn in good cognitive conditions and a corresponding bad case in which the agent does not see a barn at all but is suffering from an hallucination. Here, we would treat the agent in the good case as seeing that there is a barn before her and as also knowing this proposition, while we would treat the agent in the bad case as failing to see that there is a barn before her and as also lacking knowledge of this proposition. The very different kind of barn case cited above which concerns a misleading defeater suggests, however, that we need to rethink this simple model of good and bad cases.

I propose the following taxonomy of good and bad cases.

A Taxonomy of Good and Bad Cases

	Good+	Good	Bad	Bad+	Bad++	Bad+++
Objectively Epistemically Good?	Yes	Yes	No	No	No	No
Subjectively Epistemically Good?	Yes	No	Yes	No	Yes	No
Veridical?	Yes	Yes	Yes	Yes	No	No
Sees that *p*?	Yes	Yes	No	No	No	No
Knows that *p*?	Yes	No	No	No	No	No

In order to understand what is going on in this table we first need to explore the idea that a case can describe a scenario which is *objectively* epistemically good or bad, and also *subjectively* epistemically good or bad.

By the former contrast I have in mind facts about the nature of the environment and about the cognitive faculties of the agent in question. That the agent is in an environment which is such that even if her relevant belief-forming faculties were functioning properly she would not be in a position to reliably form true beliefs—if, for instance, she were employing her barn-detecting abilities in an environment in which most barn-shaped objects are in fact cleverly construed barn façades—would constitute an example of a scenario being objectively epistemically bad on account of a feature of the environment.[21] That the agent's relevant cognitive faculties are not functioning properly—if, for instance, she has ingested some sort of hallucinogenic drug—would constitute an example of a scenario being objectively epistemically bad on account of a feature of the subject's cognitive abilities.

In contrast, those scenarios where the agent's relevant cognitive faculties are functioning normally, and where the environment is conducive for the formation of the salient range of true beliefs, would be classed as objectively epistemically good. So described, a perceptual belief formed in objectively epistemically good circumstances is obviously bound to be true. In essence, the thinking behind our characterization of an objectively epistemically good scenario is that the agent is reliably forming her perceptual beliefs in such a manner that they will inevitably be true in environments which are suitably conducive to this belief-forming process, and that the agent is in just such an environment.

The distinction between subjectively epistemically good and bad scenarios concerns whether the agent is in possession of sufficient grounds for doubt with regard to the target proposition. The case described above of an agent who has been told by an ordinarily reliable informant that most of the barn-shaped objects in the vicinity are fakes would fall into this category, since the agent now has sufficient grounds for doubting the target proposition and indeed should not believe this proposition unless she gains additional grounds which neutralize this defeater (e.g., she gets to make further investigations regarding the barn before her, which indicate that it is not one of the barn façades). As we described this case above it was important that the ground in question was a *misleading* defeater, in that the testimony in question was in fact false. In terms of what we are now thinking of as a subjectively epistemically bad scenario, however, it wouldn't matter whether the defeater was misleading in this way; what matters is just that it is not neutralized by further grounds. In contrast, a subjectively epistemically good scenario is a scenario where no such defeater is present.[22]

One last caveat is in order in this regard: we will treat as a subjectively epistemically bad scenario any scenario in which the agent either is aware of sufficient grounds for doubt with regard to the target proposition, or *should be* aware of such grounds.[23] The latter clause is important, since we clearly do not want a scenario to count as subjectively epistemically good just because the agent—through, say, sheer inattentiveness on her part— doesn't become aware of a defeater that she should have become aware of.

Finally, a third axis along which we can distinguish cases is in terms of whether or not the perceptual belief formed in that case is veridical.

One last point of clarification is in order with regard to this taxonomy of good and bad cases. So far we have been describing such cases as being in their nature introspectively indistinguishable. Notice, however, that we will need to nuance this point a little in order to accommodate this more complex way of thinking about good and bad cases, since whether or not one is in possession of a defeater clearly can be introspectively distinguishable. We will thus say that for any particular case that you plug into this taxonomy the various scenarios will be introspectively indistinguishable in all respects other than with regard to the presence of these defeaters.

In order to clarify the different possibilities that are being mapped out by this table, it will be helpful to run through these possibilities with illustrative examples. As a template, we will use the general example of an agent seeing what she takes to be a barn and on this basis forming, where relevant, a belief that there is a barn before her (*p*).

An example of a good+ scenario would be where the agent sees a barn in good cognitive conditions (both environmental and in terms of the functioning of her relevant faculties) and believes that *p* on this basis where she is (quite properly) not aware of any grounds for doubt as regards the target proposition. This scenario is thus both objectively and subjectively epistemically good, and consequently the perception is veridical. By everyone's lights, such a case would be an example in which the agent both sees that *p* and knows that *p*. It is the good+ scenario that the epistemological disjunctivist has in mind when she talks of paradigm cases of perceptual knowledge. On this view in the good+ case the agent's perceptual knowledge is constituted by the possession of the factive rational support provided by her seeing that *p*.

An example of a merely good scenario would be one identical to that just given as an example of a good+ scenario except that the scenario is subjectively epistemically bad because the agent is in possession of (or should be in possession of) a defeater for the target proposition (acquired, say, via testimony from a reliable source). Since the scenario is objectively epistemically good it follows that the perception will be veridical. Given that this is a subjectively epistemically bad scenario, however, it also follows that the agent lacks knowledge (indeed, she shouldn't even believe the target proposition).

Still, as noted above, it does seem to be right to say that this agent sees that *p*, and thus merely good cases reveal the logical gap between seeing that *p* and knowing that *p*. That the scenario is objectively epistemically good makes clear why this is so, since the agent is, as a matter of fact, in a good position to gain knowledge of the target proposition. Her seeing that *p* in this case thus does indeed put her in an objectively good position to know that *p*. It is just that she cannot exploit this fact because of the presence of the defeater, a defeater which, since the circumstances are in fact objectively epistemically good, is necessarily misleading.

Note that while the primary basis on which seeing that *p* and knowing that *p* come apart on this view will be cases like this where the agent, though in a scenario which is objectively epistemically good, is nonetheless in possession (or ought to be in possession) of a defeater, there will also be other, more peripheral, ways in which they can come apart. These will be cases where the failure to know that p even despite seeing that p relates to an unusual feature of how the agent is in this case forming and sustaining her beliefs. One such possibility is that of the agent being in an objectively epistemically good circumstance and yet simply failing to believe that p, even though she has no subjective basis for this failure to believe. If she doesn't believe that p, then she is not even in the market for knowledge that p, and yet since the circumstances are objectively epistemically good she would on this view count as seeing that p. Indeed, wouldn't we naturally describe her as seeing that p, and hence be puzzled by her failure to believe that p in this case?

A second kind of possibility, related to the first, is that the agent believes that p without that belief being formed and sustained on the rational basis supplied by her seeing that p. For example, the belief might be formed and sustained on a non-epistemic basis (e.g., wishful thinking), or formed and sustained on an inadequate epistemic basis (e.g., on the basis of evidence which is insufficient to support knowledge that p). Again, since the agent is in an objectively epistemically good scenario she counts on this view as seeing that p, but she clearly does not know that p given how her belief was formed. Since cases like this depend upon oddities about the agent's doxastic practices, we will in what follows focus our attention in our discussion on merely good cases of the more central type involving misleading defeaters.

An example of a merely bad scenario would be where the agent genuinely sees a barn in a scenario in which what looks like a barn generally is not a barn (e.g., in barn façade county). The circumstances would thus be objectively epistemically bad. Nonetheless, since there is no defeater that the agent is or should be aware of the circumstances are subjectively epistemically good, and the perception is also veridical since she really does see a barn. Still, that the circumstances are objectively epistemically bad ensures that the agent lacks knowledge that p, even while forming a true belief that p. In particular, it ensures that the agent's cognitive success is merely a matter of luck, and so is not in the market for knowledge.[24] Relatedly, it also explains why the agent does not see that p in this case for, as a matter of fact, she is not in circumstances that put her in a good position to know this proposition, and so the essential epistemic link that we have described between seeing that *p* and knowing that *p* is not satisfied.[25]

An example of a bad+ scenario would be one that is exactly like that just described except that the agent in addition has grounds for doubting the target proposition. She is thus in a scenario which is both objectively and subjectively epistemically bad. Nonetheless, as it happens her perception is veridical, in that she does see a barn. Perhaps, for instance, most barn-shaped objects in this vicinity are not barns and she has been told this, and yet she just so happens to be looking at the one real barn in the area. Clearly our agent neither knows that *p* in this case nor sees that *p*. Indeed, she shouldn't even believe that *p* in this case.

An example of a bad++ scenario would be a case identical to a merely bad case except that the perception was not veridical. That is, the agent is in an objectively epistemically bad scenario and in addition merely seems to see a barn rather than actually seeing one. For example, it could be that she is in barn façade county and has the added misfortune of being the victim of an hallucination of a barn. Clearly our agent neither knows that *p* in this case nor sees that *p*.

An example of a bad+++ scenario would be a case identical to a bad++ case except that in addition the agent is aware, or should be aware, of a defeater for her belief that *p*. Her belief is thus formed in circumstances that are both objectively and subjectively epistemically bad, and her perception is also not veridical. For example, perhaps in addition to being in barn façade county and being the victim of an hallucination she is also given good reason for supposing that she is hallucinating (perhaps she has been told by a reliable informant that this is the case). Clearly our agent neither knows that *p* in this case nor sees that *p*. Indeed, as in the merely bad case, she shouldn't even believe that *p* in this case.

A crucial point about this taxonomy of good and bad cases is that it offers us a way of thinking about the relationship between seeing that *p* and knowing that *p* which affords us a straightforward response to the basis problem. For while on this view we can accommodate the intuition that underlies the entailment thesis that seeing that *p* is both factive and strongly epistemic—since one only sees that *p* in cases of veridical perception which are objectively epistemically advantageous—we are not forced thereby into accepting the entailment thesis, and thus holding that seeing that *p* entails knowing that *p*. But once we jettison the entailment thesis, there is then nothing to prevent us from allowing that seeing that

p can be the rational basis for knowing that p. By guaranteeing that you are in an objective epistemically good scenario and that one's perception is veridical, seeing that p ensures that from an objective point of view you are in a good position to know that p. Crucially, however, it does not guarantee you knowledge that p. The basis problem for epistemological disjunctivism is thus neutralized.[26]

§6. Epistemological Disjunctivism and the Epistemic Externalism/ Internalism Distinction

As we noted in the introduction, part of the great promise of epistemological disjunctivism lies in its apparent ability to incorporate key insights from both sides of the epistemic externalism/internalism distinction. In order to locate the view within the contemporary debate regarding this distinction, however, we first need to radically rethink the framework of this debate.

Consider the classical tripartite account of knowledge as justified true belief. This is typically characterized as a paradigm internalist view about knowledge, and the reason for this is that the justification condition which converts mere true belief into knowledge is clearly an internalist epistemic condition (we will examine what it is about this condition that makes it an internalist epistemic condition in a moment). So the standard story goes, Gettier-style cases conclusively demonstrate that the classical account of knowledge is fatally flawed, and hence that a certain type of epistemic internalism about knowledge is refuted.[27]

While the Gettier-style cases are standardly thought to refute a certain kind of internalism about knowledge, they are not held to undermine all internalist views about knowledge. In particular, post-Gettier, epistemic internalism is normally interpreted as holding only that a core prerequisite for knowledge is the satisfaction of an internal epistemic condition, such as a justification condition (where justification is conceived along epistemic internalist lines). So, for example, while epistemic internalists no longer hold that knowledge is just justified true belief, they might well continue to maintain that it is *at least* justified true belief.

In contrast, externalist views about knowledge deny this claim and so argue that it is possible for an agent to have knowledge even while failing to satisfy a substantive internal epistemic condition.[28] Indeed, they will typically claim that such 'animal' knowledge which does not involve the satisfaction of a substantive internal epistemic condition is in fact fairly common. So, for example, a process reliabilist account of knowledge might hold that an agent can gain knowledge simply by forming a belief via a reliable process, where the reliability condition in play here is clearly not an internal epistemic condition.[29]

What is it about an epistemic condition that makes it an *internal* epistemic condition? Typically, internal epistemic conditions are characterized in terms of a reflective access requirement. So, for example, in the classical account of knowledge the justification condition is an internalist condition because whether one is justified in one's beliefs is held to be something that the agent can determine by reflection alone. More generally, we can offer the following formulation of the *accessibilist* account of internal epistemic support:

Accessibilism
S's internalist epistemic support for believing that ϕ is constituted solely by facts that S can know by reflection alone.

So, for example, that one's belief has been formed via a reliable belief-forming process will not form part of the *internalist* epistemic support you have for this belief by accessibilist lights, since this is not a fact that is reflectively accessible to one. At most, then, such a consideration can offer only *externalist* epistemic support.[30]

More recently, however, defenders of epistemic internalism have put forward a different characterization of what makes an epistemic condition internal. According to this view, known as *mentalism*, the degree of internalist epistemic support one possesses is determined by one's mental states.[31] We can formulate this view as follows:

Mentalism
S's internalist epistemic support for believing that ϕ is constituted solely by S's mental states.

As with accessibilism, the kind of factors relevant to epistemic standing typically advocated by the epistemic externalist will not satisfy this principle. As before, consider process reliabilism in this regard. This principle entails that two agents who are alike in terms of their mental states will also be alike in terms of the internalist epistemic support that their beliefs enjoy. Nonetheless, one of the agents might well be forming her beliefs in ways that are more reliable than the other agent, and if so then by process reliabilist lights these agents will not be alike in terms of the specifically externalist epistemic support that their beliefs enjoy.

Depending on one's view about mental states, there may not be an extensional difference between these two proposals regarding how best to characterize epistemic internalism. If it is only one's mental states that are reflectively accessible to one, and if one's mental states are always reflectively accessible, then two counterpart agents will not differ in the degree of internalist epistemic support they have on either view. The further theses required to make these two views extensionally equivalent in this way are, however, controversial, and so it is important to keep these two accounts separate.

Epistemological disjunctivism explicitly describes paradigm cases of perceptual knowledge—i.e., perceptual knowledge which is gained in good+ cases, as outlined above—as essentially involving rational support which satisfies a reflective access requirement. Epistemological disjunctivism is thus committed to accessibilism. In paradigm cases of perceptual knowledge, two agents who are identical in terms of what they are able to know by reflection alone would on the epistemological disjunctivist view also be identical in terms of the internalist epistemic support that they have for their beliefs, in line with accessibilism. For example, in both cases they will have reflective access to the rational support provided by their seeing that p and so will enjoy equal levels of internalist epistemic support for their respective beliefs that p.

Whether epistemological disjunctivism is committed to mentalism depends on whether you count an agent's seeing that p as a mental state. If you do—and this proposal will seem plausible to some[32]—then it will follow that in paradigm cases of perceptual knowledge two agents who are identical in their mental states will on the epistemological disjunctivist view also be identical in the internalist epistemic support they have for their beliefs, in line with mentalism. In both cases, they will be in the mental state of seeing that p and so will possess an identical degree of rational epistemic support as a result. Note that allying epistemological disjunctivism to mentalism in this way may require one to also endorse metaphysical disjunctivism. At the very least, the most natural view on which seeing that p counts as a mental state would surely be a metaphysically disjunctivist view. But the crux of the matter is that there is no essential tension between epistemological disjunctivism and mentalism.[33]

Given that accessibilism and mentalism are the two main ways of characterizing internal epistemic conditions, this leads to a puzzle. After all, standard internalist theories of knowledge are robustly opposed to epistemological disjunctivism in that they do not allow there to be reflectively accessible factive reasons for believing specific empirical propositions. But if epistemological disjunctivism can potentially satisfy the accessibilist and mentalist rubrics to the same extent as standard epistemic internalist views, then it is hard to see why this position shouldn't count as a standard version of epistemic internalism as well, albeit one that is specifically concerned with paradigm cases of perceptual knowledge.

In order to draw out the sense in which epistemological disjunctivism is a non-standard internalist epistemological theory, we need to consider a claim which is widely held to be core to epistemic internalism, to the extent that it is typically endorsed by both mentalists and accessibilists. This is the so-called 'new evil genius' thesis, and it can be characterized as follows:

The New Evil Genius Thesis
S's internalist epistemic support for believing that ϕ is constituted solely by properties that S has in common with her recently envatted physical duplicate.[34]

Like the sceptical use of envatment, the recently envatted physical duplicate at issue here has experiences which are introspectively indistinguishable from the experiences of her non-envatted counterpart. It is for this reason that it is held to be the case that the non-envatted subject cannot be any better off, epistemically speaking, than her envatted counterpart.

The kind of epistemic support typically appealed to by epistemic externalists will not satisfy this thesis. Consider process reliabilism again. Whether or not one is envatted can obviously have implications for whether one's beliefs have been formed via reliable processes, and hence can by process reliabilist lights have a bearing on the extent to which one's beliefs enjoy epistemic support. But clearly by the lights of the new evil genius thesis such 'external' considerations cannot have a bearing on the degree of internalist epistemic support that one's beliefs enjoy.[35]

Given that accessibilists and mentalists will typically endorse the new evil genius thesis, one might naturally wonder how these three theses are related. Let's take first the relationship between accessibilism and the new evil genius thesis. Consider the following argument:

From Accessibilism to the New Evil Genius Thesis

(1) *S*'s internalist epistemic support for believing that *p* is constituted solely by facts that *S* can know by reflection alone. [Accessibilism]

(2) The only facts that *S* can know by reflection alone are facts that *S*'s recently envatted physical duplicate can also know by reflection alone. [Premise]

(C) *S*'s internalist epistemic support for believing that *p* is constituted solely by properties that *S* has in common with her recently envatted physical duplicate. [The New Evil Genius Thesis; from (1), (2)]

(1) is simply the accessibilist thesis, and the conclusion is of course just the new evil genius thesis. I take it that (1) and (2) uncontentiously entail the conclusion. The dialectical weight of this argument thus falls on the additional premise in play—i.e., (2). Put simply, if this premise is true, then there is a straightforward way of deriving the new evil genius thesis from accessibilism.

I take it that most contemporary epistemologists—whether epistemic externalists or internalists—will be inclined to accept (2). Given that, *ex hypothesi*, one's experiences in the vat are indistinguishable from one's experiences outside of the vat, then many will find it natural to suppose that there can be nothing which is reflectively accessible to the unenvatted subject that isn't also available to her recently envatted physical duplicate. And yet it is precisely a claim of this sort which is rejected by epistemological disjunctivism. In particular, the epistemological disjunctivist holds that there are facts which are reflectively accessible to the subject (at least in good+ cases), such as that she sees that such-and-such is the case, which are not reflectively accessible to her recently envatted physical duplicate.

What about the relationship between mentalism and the new evil genius thesis? If mentalism entails accessibilism, then of course the above argument from accessibilism to the new evil genius thesis could be easily supplemented so as to offer us an argumentative route from mentalism to the new evil genius thesis. But, as noted above, the logical relationship between mentalism and accessibilism is moot, and so we cannot take such an entailment for granted.

With this point in mind, consider the following argument:

From Mentalism to the New Evil Genius Thesis
(1★)   S's internalist epistemic support for believing that p is constituted solely by S's mental states. [Mentalism]

(2★)   S and S's recently envatted physical duplicate have mental states that are essentially the same. [Premise]

(C★)   S's internalist epistemic support for believing that p is constituted solely by properties that S has in common with her recently envatted physical duplicate. [The New Evil Genius Thesis; from (1★), (2★)]

(1★) is simply the mentalist thesis, and the conclusion—(C★)—is just the new evil genius thesis. As before, then, everything hangs on the additional premise in play—i.e., in this case (2★)—at least insofar as (1★) and (2★) entail (C★). But is it obvious that (1★) and (2★) entail (C★)? As it stands, I don't think so. Instead, this rests on how we are interpreting (2★).

Let's look again at (2★). Note that the claim is not that S and her recently envatted physical duplicate have exactly the same mental states (which certainly would be contentious), but just that they are 'essentially' the same. Everything thus hangs on the 'essentially' in play here. I take it that we are meant to be reading (2★) in such a way that what differences there are when it comes to S's mental states and those of her recently envatted physical duplicate are negligible to the extent that, from the mentalist perspective at least, they make no difference to the internalist epistemic standing of these subjects' beliefs. So read, (2★) is certainly able to entail, in conjunction with (1★), the conclusion of this argument, (C★).

Is (2★), so construed, a plausible claim? My hunch is that those attracted to mentalism will find this claim plausible—even though it isn't in any way entailed by the view—and that this is why mentalists tend to endorse the new evil genius thesis. We noted above that epistemological disjunctivism is incompatible with (2). Is there a similar incompatibility with (2★)? Well, potentially there is, at least if we interpret epistemological disjunctivism such that seeing that p is a mental state. On this interpretation, S and her recently envatted physical duplicate can indeed have significantly different mental states, where this difference has important epistemological ramifications. Epistemological disjunctivism so construed is thus incompatible with (2★). This will be because S (in good+ cases at least) will have the mental states of seeing that certain facts obtain, while her recently envatted physical duplicate will lack these mental states.

So epistemological disjunctivism is committed to accessibilism, but represents a non-standard version of accessibilism in that it rejects the new evil genius thesis, and rejects it because it denies (2). Moreover, insofar as epistemological disjunctivism is committed to mentalism, then it is again a non-standard version of mentalism on account of its rejection of the new evil genius thesis. In this case its rejection of the new evil genius thesis reflects the fact that a mentalist rendering of epistemological disjunctivism is committed to denying (2★). Given that it is moot whether epistemological disjunctivism is wedded to mentalism, but that it is not moot that epistemological disjunctivism is wedded to accessibilism, in what follows we will focus on the epistemological disjunctivist's rejection of (2).[36]

It is important to notice that the epistemological disjunctivist's grounds for denying (2) in fact license the denial of an even stronger thesis than that expressed by (2). For on the epistemological disjunctivist account it is not just subjects and their recently envatted physical duplicates who differ in terms of the facts that they can access by reflection alone. Indeed, any pairing of a good+ case with a corresponding bad case can be used to make the point, even if the agent in the target bad case is not a recently envatted physical duplicate (i.e., any one of the types of 'bad' case delineated above can be used in this regard). What's important is just that the agent in the good+ case sees that certain facts obtain, while the agent in the corresponding bad case, while having experiences which are introspectively indistinguishable from the experiences had by her counterpart, does not see that these facts obtain.[37]

In general, then, epistemological disjunctivists don't just deny (2), but also a stronger thesis, which we will christen—for reasons that will soon become apparent—the *highest common factor thesis*:

The Highest Common Factor Thesis
The only facts that S can know by reflection alone in a good+ case are facts that S's physical duplicate in a corresponding bad case can also know by reflection alone.

That is, what epistemological disjunctivists are resisting is the idea that just because good+ cases and corresponding bad cases are introspectively indistinguishable, it follows that the facts that the subject has reflective access to in the good+ case are no different from the facts that the subject has reflective access to in the corresponding bad case. The example of a subject and her recently envatted physical duplicate is just an instance of a good+ case and a corresponding bad case which can be used to make this point.

Does this mean that epistemological disjunctivists are committed to rejecting the intuitions which drive the new evil genius thesis out of hand? If so, then that would be a problem for epistemological disjuncti- vism, since the view could then be charged with being unable to accom- modate the core guiding intuitions of epistemic internalism (the new evil genius thesis, after all, is typically endorsed by both accessibilists and mentalists). Fortunately, help is at hand for the epistemological disjuncti- vist on this score.

Recall that the new evil genius thesis is formulated in such a way that the subject's internalist epistemic support for her beliefs is constituted *solely* by properties that this subject shares with her recently envatted physical duplicate. As we have seen, epistemological disjunctivists are committed to rejecting this thesis, since on this view a subject's internalist epistemic support for her beliefs can be very different depending on whether she is envatted. But that doesn't mean that epistemological disjunctivists are obliged to argue that there isn't an internalist epistemic standing which is common to both the subject and her envatted duplicate. In particular, it is widely noted about the subjects in the new evil genius example that one epistemic standing that they share is that they are equally *blameless* in believing as they do. After all, by hypothesis it is impossible for an agent to introspectively distinguish between normal experiences and the experi- ences had once placed in the vat, so on what basis could one blame the envatted agent for having fewer true beliefs than her unenvatted counter- part?

It is thus open to the epistemological disjunctivist to argue that what is driving the new evil genius thesis is the fact that the two agents concerned are equally epistemically blameless in believing as they do. That the two agents are equally epistemically blameless, however, does not entail that they enjoy equal levels of internalist epistemic support, or that a subject's internalist epistemic support is constituted solely by properties that she has in common with her recently envatted physical duplicate. In this way, the epistemological disjunctivist can accommodate the intuitions driving the new evil genius thesis while nonetheless rejecting this claim.[38]

More generally, the epistemological disjunctivist can extend this line of reasoning to examples involving good+ and corresponding bad cases. While the epistemological disjunctivist is committed to denying that the subjects in such cases enjoy identical levels of internalist epistemic support for their beliefs, they can nonetheless hold that there is an epistemic standing which is common to both subjects. For given that good+ cases and corresponding bad cases are *ex hypothesi* introspectively indistinguishable, it follows that, just as in the pair of cases at issue in the new evil genius thesis, the agents concerned will be likewise equally blameless in believing as they do.[39]

Understanding that epistemological disjunctivists reject the highest common factor thesis is crucial to seeing why they resist a train of argument that John McDowell (e.g., 1995) describes as the 'highest common factor' argument. We can represent this argument as follows, where for the 'bad' case any type of bad case of the sort described in our taxonomy above will do:

The Highest Common Factor Argument

(HC1) In a bad case, the rational support for one's belief is weaker than factive rational support. [Premise]

(HC2) One is unable to introspectively distinguish between the good+ case and a corresponding bad case. [Premise]

(HCC1) The rational support that one has in favour of one's belief in the good+ case can be no better than it is in a corresponding bad case. [From (HC2)]

(HCC2) In the good+ case, the rational support for one's belief is weaker than factive epistemic support. [From (HC1), (HCC1)]

Clearly, epistemological disjunctivists will want to object to this train of reasoning. The problem, however, is to put one's finger on precisely what is wrong with it, since each step seems perfectly sound. In particular, the two premises seem undeniable, and moreover would be endorsed by the epistemological disjunctivist. Clearly, it is also undeniable that the intermediate conclusion and the first premise—i.e., (HCC1) and (HC1)—entail the ultimate conclusion, (HCC2). The joker in the pack must thus be the inference from the second premise, (HC2), to the intermediate conclusion.

Given the foregoing discussion, I think we can identify what is problematic about this inference. For by epistemological disjunctivist lights the most that will follow from the fact that the good+ case and the corresponding bad case are introspectively indistinguishable is that the agents concerned are equally epistemically blameless in holding their beliefs.[40] But *that* claim falls well short of the intermediate conclusion, and hence the argument doesn't go through. What the proponent of the highest common factor argument needs to make the argument valid is a much stronger premise than (HC2). Indeed, what she needs is the disputed highest common factor thesis.

In order to see this, consider this reformulated version of the highest common factor argument, where the highest common factor thesis is substituted for (HC2):

The Reformulated Highest Common Factor Argument
(HC1′) In a bad case, the rational support for one's belief is weaker than factive rational support. [Premise]

(HC2′) The only facts that one can know by reflection alone in a good+ case are facts that one's physical duplicate in a corresponding bad case can also know by reflection alone. [The Highest Common Factor Thesis]

(HCC1′) The rational support that one has in favour of one's belief in the good+ case can be no better than it is in a corresponding bad case. [From (HC2′)]

(HCC2′) In the good+ case, the rational support for one's belief is weaker than factive epistemic support. [From (HC1′), (HCC1′)]

Given that epistemological disjunctivists are committed to accessibilism, one can straightforwardly derive the intermediate conclusion from the revised second premise in this argument. For insofar as the facts that are reflectively accessible to the subjects in the good+ case and the corresponding bad case are the same, then it follows (given accessibilism) that the agent in the good+ case cannot have a better rational basis for her belief than her counterpart in the bad case. The highest common factor thesis thus entails, given accessibilism, (HCC1′). And since it is not in dispute that the intermediate conclusion, in conjunction with the first premise, entails the ultimate conclusion of this argument, the argument is now valid.

But while the epistemological disjunctivist will certainly grant the validity of this argument, they will contend that it is unsound, since the key premise—i.e., the highest common factor thesis—is something that that they explicitly deny. In the work of McDowell this point that there is a lacuna in the highest common factor argument is largely negative, in the sense that his main goal is just to show that the conclusion reached in this argument is not compulsory in the way that it is typically presented, and hence that the path is laid open for epistemological disjunctivism (a view that he regards as 'sheer common sense', which is only in doubt because 'questionable philosophy [... has] put it at risk' (McDowell 2002a, 98)). The problem with this negative strategy, however, is that there are some standing concerns about the plausibility of rational support in the perceptual case which is both factive and reflectively accessible. Indeed, we noted three such concerns above. But it is precisely due to the epistemological disjunctivist's commitment to there being factive and reflectively accessible rational support available in the perceptual case that they reject the highest common factor thesis. It is thus vital that we neutralize these three worries about rational support which is both factive and reflectively accessible if we are to have a response to the highest common factor argument which is fully satisfying.

We have dealt with one of these three problems facing epistemological disjunctivism above (the basis problem), and in the next section we will conclude part one by dealing with a second of these problems (the access problem). In part two we will introduce some further epistemological machinery in order to deal with the final outstanding problem (the distinguishability problem). With these three objections to the idea of reflectively accessible factive rational support in the perceptual case neutralized— and bearing in mind the theoretical advantages that epistemological disjunctivism has over its rivals, as set out in the introduction—we will be in a much stronger position to maintain that epistemological disjunctivists can rightly reject the highest common factor thesis and thus resist the highest common factor argument.

§7. Resolving the Access Problem

We will start by stating the problematic argument at issue in the access problem more explicitly. This can be done as follows:

The Access Problem

(AP1) S can know by reflection alone that her reason for believing the specific empirical proposition p is the factive reason R. [Premise]

(AP2) S can know by reflection alone that R entails p. [Premise]

(APC) S can know by reflection alone the specific empirical proposition p. [From (AP1), (AP2)]

(AP1) is a direct consequence of the epistemological disjunctivist thesis, since this holds that the factive reasons one possesses in support of one's perceptual knowledge in paradigm cases are reflectively accessible, where this means that one can know that one possesses this factive rational support by reflection alone. So, for example, if one has paradigmatic perceptual knowledge that p, then one can know by reflection alone that one's reason for believing that p is that one sees that p. (AP2) simply expresses the uncontentious truth that one can come to know by purely reflective means that factive reasons entail the propositions that they are reasons for. So, for example, one can come to know by reflection alone that seeing that p entails p. But given (AP1) and (AP2), then the conclusion (APC) seems to immediately follow, and yet this conclusion would be intellectually disastrous for epistemological disjunctivism, since it would commit this view to the idea that it is possible to know specific empirical propositions by reflection alone.

Imagine, for example, that the p in question is that there is a barn in the field, where one is in a good+ case in which one sees that this is so and has knowledge of this proposition on this basis. Is it really plausible to suppose that simply by reflecting on one's rational support for one's belief that *p*, and on the nature of factive reasons, that one could *thereby* come to know this empirical proposition (i.e., come to know, by reflection alone, that there is a barn in the field)?

Fortunately for epistemological disjunctivism, the access problem does not present a challenge to the view because the conclusion of the above argument, (APC), fails to follow from the premises, contrary to first appearances. In order to see this, it will be helpful if we examine more closely the specific instance of the access problem just described:

The Access Problem'

(AP1') *S* can know by reflection alone that her reason for believing that there is a barn before her is the factive reason that she sees that there is a barn before her. [Premise]

(AP2') *S* can know by reflection alone that if she sees that there is a barn in front of her, then there is a barn in front of her. [Premise]

(APC') *S* can know by reflection alone that there is a barn in front of her. [From (AP1'), (AP2')]

Now look again at the first premise, (AP1'). With an example plugged into the access problem, we can see that given the nature of the first premise there is in fact something very puzzling about the conclusion of this argument. This is because this premise specifically states that *S*'s reason for believing that there is a barn before her is the *empirical* reason that she *sees that* there is a barn before her. But if that's right, then it is odd that *S* can use the reasoning in play here to derive the conclusion that she can know *by reflection alone* that there is a barn before her. After all, it is explicit in the first premise that *S*'s route to her acquisition of this (putatively) exclusively reflective knowledge of the target proposition essentially depends on the fact that she has empirical reason to believe this proposition.

Note that the worry being raised here is not that one cannot come to have exclusively reflective knowledge of a proposition in cases where one already has an empirical basis for believing that proposition, since this is clearly false. For example, suppose that one's only epistemic basis for believing a certain mathematical proposition is empirical, such as testimony from a reliable colleague. Now imagine that one subsequently conducts what is clearly a competent proof which establishes this proposition beyond doubt. One will now know the target proposition, but while the empirical epistemic support is still present, it will normally be the case that one's belief in the target proposition will now be based on the competent proof rather than on this additional epistemic support. After all, this competent proof offers one sufficient (indeed, *overwhelming*) epistemic support for this knowledge, such that if one were to lose the additional empirical epistemic support—if one were to lose faith in the reliability of one's colleague when it comes to mathematical matters, say—then one could still continue to knowledgably believe the target proposition on the non-empirical basis provided by the proof. The epistemic basis for the knowledge in question can thus be exclusively reflective, even despite the fact that one might well have additional empirical epistemic support for this belief and, indeed, additional empirical epistemic support which pre-dates the reflective epistemic support that one has for this belief which is supplied by the proof.

Accordingly, it had better not be the case that the difficulty we are raising for the access problem trades on the idea that one cannot come to have exclusively reflective knowledge of a proposition in cases where one already has an empirical basis for believing that proposition. Fortunately for us, it doesn't. For notice that the challenge we are posing for the access problem is in fact far more specific. In the case just described where one moves from having empirical epistemic support to having (overwhelming) reflective epistemic support, and where one comes to knows on this latter basis alone, what is key is that one is no longer *basing* one's belief on the empirical epistemic support once the competent proof has been conducted. Indeed, it is only if this is so that the resultant knowledge is properly classed as exclusively reflective.

If, for example, one's confidence in the competence of the proof in part rests on that prior empirical epistemic support—for instance, if one has qualms about the competence of the proof, and one would not have usually formed a belief on the basis of it, but one sets aside those qualms purely because of the testimonial grounds previously acquired—then clearly we wouldn't want to say that one's knowledge is now exclusively reflective. For it would now be based in part on the empirical epistemic support that one has for this proposition. (And notice that given how we have just described the case, if one lost the empirical epistemic support then one would certainly thereby lose one's knowledge, since one would no longer even believe the target proposition.)

Crucially, however, the challenge we are raising for the access problem explicitly concerns a case where the agent continues to *base* her belief on the prior empirical epistemic support that she has. For it remains true throughout the inference in play in the access problem that the epistemic basis for S's belief that there is a barn before her at least includes the empirical epistemic support that she sees that there is a barn before her. Indeed, it is not a contingent matter that this be so, since it is only if this is the case that the first premise of the argument is true (and, of course, if the first premise is not true then the argument doesn't go through anyway).

Now one might think that the proponent of the access problem can easily evade this response, since it seems that all they need to do is reformulate the first premise so that while the agent is in possession of the factive reason, it is not the basis on which they believe the target proposition. After all, we noted above (§5) that epistemological disjunctivism explicitly allows that in merely good cases it is possible that an agent might see that p while failing to believe that p. Accordingly, in such cases the subject is presumably in a position to know by reflection alone that she is in possession of the factive reason even while not believing the target proposition on this basis. Hence, the access problem will go through after all, since one cannot now object to the problematic conclusion being derived on the grounds that the knowledge in question cannot be exclusively reflective.

Here, then, is the proposed reformulation of the access problem such that, putatively, it can evade the line of response that we have just set out:

The Access Problem″

(AP1″) S can know by reflection alone that she is in possession of the factive reason R for believing the specific empirical proposition p (although she does not believe that p on this basis, or on any other empirical basis). [Premise]

(AP2″) S can know by reflection alone that R entails p. [Premise]

(APC″) S can know by reflection alone the specific empirical proposition p. [From (AP1″), (AP2″)]

Notice that the changes made only concern the first premise, which now makes it clear that while the agent is in possession of the factive empirical reason, this is not the basis for her belief in the target proposition. Note that I have also added the caveat that the agent does not believe the target proposition on any other empirical basis either, since this makes it completely explicit that the point behind this formulation is to block the suggestion that the conclusion does not go through because the belief in the target proposition is based on empirical rational support. Worryingly, however, these changes to the first premise don't on the face of it undermine the inference in play, and hence it appears that the access problem is indeed resurrected.

Although superficially plausible, the argument of this reformulated access problem does not go through. The problem lies with the first premise, which is false. For although the proponent of this reformulated access problem is quite right that seeing that p can come apart from believing that p in just the way specified, the manner in which this happens won't, on closer inspection, lend support to this argument.

In order to see this, consider the example of a merely good case that we offered above. This involved an agent in epistemically favourable circumstances but who was in possession of a misleading defeater which she couldn't defeat. Accordingly, while she did see that there was a barn before her, and hence was necessarily in a good position to know that there was a barn before her, she could not properly believe this proposition, and hence could not know it either. In order for this case to be such that it offers us a potential instance of the claim at issue in the first premise, then it is of course important that the agent does not inappropriately form the belief in the target proposition on the basis of the factive reason, so let's add that detail to the example as well. And let's also stipulate that she doesn't believe the target proposition on any other empirical basis either. In line with the situation set out in (AP1''), we thus have an agent who sees that there is a barn before her and yet does not believe that there is a barn before her on the basis of her seeing that this is the case (nor on any other empirical basis either).

Here is the crux. In such a case there seems no reason at all for the epistemological disjunctivist to concede that the agent concerned has reflective access to the factive reason. Their claim, after all, is only that the rational basis for your beliefs—i.e., the reasons on which one's beliefs are based—needs to be reflectively accessible. But in the case just described the factive reason is explicitly *not* a reason on which the agent's belief is based. Moreover, although the epistemological disjunctivist is willing to part company with the philosophical herd and claim that one's seeing that p can be reflectively accessible to one in cases where one has paradigmatic perceptual knowledge that p (such that one believes that p on the basis of seeing that p), it does not follow from this trail-blazing stance that they are thereby committed to supposing that in *every* case where one sees that p it is reflectively accessible to one that this is so. In particular, it does not follow that one's seeing that p should be reflectively accessible to one in cases which are epistemically sub-optimal in some way and so don't involve (paradigmatic) perceptual knowledge that p.

Indeed, in epistemically sub-optimal cases like the one just described the standard epistemological line on reflectively accessible reasons for perceptual belief, such that one's seeing that p is *not* reflectively accessible, seems perfectly sensible. A key motif of epistemological disjunctivism, after all, is that we shouldn't judge the good cases—i.e., the good+ cases—by the lights of the not-so-good cases, and the merely good case, while not quite a bad case, is certainly a not-so-good case. Accordingly, by parity of reasoning, why should allowing that one's factive empirical reasons are reflectively accessible in the good+ case entail that they are equally reflectively accessible in the merely good case? In any case, the key point is that epistemological disjunctivists are not at all committed to the idea that one's seeing that p is reflectively accessible in the relevant (merely good) cases (in this, they can agree with everyone else), and hence by epistemological disjunctivist lights the first premise of the reformulated access problem is simply false.[41]

So the reasoning at issue in the access problem is revealed to be fallacious, in that for the premises to be true it simply cannot be the case that S's knowledge of the target proposition is exclusively reflective. So what does follow from these premises? Well, I think that once we are clear that it is crucial to the argument that S's reason for believing the target proposition is an *empirical* reason, and once we are also clear that epistemological disjunctivism is only committed to the idea that one can have reflective access to one's factive empirical reasons in the good+ case, then it becomes patent that the most that can be derived from these premises is not the troubling (for the epistemological disjunctivist) conclusion that one can have exclusively reflective knowledge of a specific empirical proposition, but rather just (APC'''):

The Access Problem'''

(AP1''') In the good+ case, S can know by reflection alone that her reason for believing the specific empirical proposition p is the factive empirical reason R. [Premise]

(AP2''') S can know by reflection alone that R entails p. [Premise]

(APC''') In the good+ case, S can know by reflection alone that her reason for believing the specific empirical proposition p is the factive empirical reason R which entails p. [From (AP1'''), (AP2''')]

Again, the only change (as regards the premises anyway) is with the first premise, which now makes explicit that it is only in the good+ case that the relevant factive empirical reason is reflectively available to the subject. In keeping with this change to the first premise, the conclusion (APC‴) similarly makes explicit that it is only in the good+ case that the agent can come to know by reflection alone that the rational support available to her is factive.

There is nothing at all worrying about (APC‴) from an epistemological disjunctivist point of view, since it simply extracts one consequence of this proposal. That is, (APC‴) merely highlights that if you allow, with epistemological disjunctivism, that subjects can have reflective access to their factive empirical reasons (in the good+ case anyway), then subjects who in addition know (by reflection) what it means for an empirical reason to be factive are also thereby in a position to know by reflection alone that they are in possession of a factive empirical reason which entails the target proposition. But that claim, as we have seen, is very different from the claim that such agents can acquire knowledge of specific empirical propositions by reflection alone.

So the access problem for epistemological disjunctivism is neutralized, since the problematic conclusion in question is never generated. Given that we have also seen that one of the other key *prima facie* problems for epistemological disjunctivism—the basis problem—is similarly ineffective, we are well on our way towards demonstrating that this proposal—and in particular, this proposal's endorsement of factive reflectively accessible reasons—has far more going for it than at first meets the eye. In order to make further progress on this score, and thereby resolve the remaining *prima facie* problem for epistemological disjunctivism that we have identified (the distinguishability problem), we need to introduce an important epistemological distinction between favouring and discriminating epistemic support. This will be the topic of part two.

Notes to Part One

1. Note too that it is specifically *visual* perceptual knowledge that we will be focusing upon.

2. For a key defence of such an 'accessibilist' conception of rational support, see Chisholm (1977). See also BonJour (1985, ch. 2). Note that I'm bracketing here the potential difficulties that might be caused for this conception of rational support by Williamson's 'anti-luminosity' argument (see Williamson 1996a; 2000a, ch. 4). I think the jury is out regarding what this argument precisely demonstrates, but in any case the proponent of the claim that rational support must be reflectively accessible needs to either rebut this argument or else demonstrate that it is compatible with its conclusions. For two useful recent critical discussions of Williamson's argument, see Brueckner and Fiocco (2002) and Berker (2008). See also Steup (2009) and Tennant (2009), to which Williamson (2009) responds.

3. A more nuanced account of 'good' and 'bad' cases is offered below. I interpret 'introspective indistinguishability' in what I take to be the standard way, such that it concerns an inability on the part of the agent to tell (= know) by introspection alone that case α is non-identical to case β. Note that this relation is explicitly relativized to the agent concerned, and hence is not to be read impersonally or in an idealized fashion. I take this relation to be reflexive and symmetric. Such a relation is unlikely to be transitive, however, and if so then it will not be an equivalence relation (though see Halpern (2008) for an opposing view on this score). For two useful discussions of the non-transitivity of introspective indistinguishability, and some of the issues this raises in the context of (metaphysical) disjunctivism, see Hawthorne and Kovakovich (2006) and Sturgeon (2006).

4. Or, at least, that what differences there are in the degree of reflectively accessible rational support available to the two subjects, they are *indistinguishable* differences.

5. That epistemological disjunctivism occupies a kind of default position in our thinking about perceptual knowledge, on account of its being rooted in a commonsense picture of our rational support for such knowledge, is a recurring theme in the work of McDowell. Consider, for example, the following passage:

> My main point in 'Knowledge and the Internal' [McDowell 1995] is to protest against the interiorization of the justifications available to us for claims about the external world. The interiorization threatens to deprive us of the justificatory power of, for instance, the form 'I see that . . .' I insist that statements of such forms are proper moves in the game of giving reasons, and their truth fully vindicates entitlement to the embedded proposition. This ought to seem sheer common sense, and it would if questionable philosophy did not put it at risk. (McDowell 2002a, 98)

6. I consider this possibility in detail in Pritchard (2003).

7. See McKinsey (1991). For a recent set of discussions of this tension between first-person authority and content externalism, Nuccetelli (2003).

8. See, for example, Williamson (2000a, ch. 1) and Cassam (2007a; 2007b). See also Dretske (1969, 78–139).

9. There are also other disjunctivist views outside the philosophy of perception, such as regarding action, though obviously they fall outwith our present concerns. See, for example, Dancy (2008), Hornsby (2008), and Ruben (2008).

10. Just as there are other possible views that might fall under the general epistemological disjunctivist label. See also endnote 13.

11. Of course, they share the negative epistemological property of being introspectively indistinguishable, but this is not usually regarded as a plausible candidate for being a property which determines the essential nature of the relevant experiences.

12. For an excellent survey of the range of metaphysical disjunctivist positions on offer in the literature, see Soteriou (2009). See also Haddock and Macpherson (2008b), Byrne and Logue (2009b), Fish (2009), Brogaard (2010), and Dorsch (2011). For some of the key defences of metaphysical disjunctivism, see Hinton (1967a; 1967b; 1973), Snowdon (1980–1; 1990–1), and Martin (2002; 2004; 2006). See also the papers collected in Haddock and Macpherson (2008a) and Byrne and Logue (2009a). For an important recent exchange on metaphysical disjunctivism, see Hawthorne and Kovakovich (2006) and Sturgeon (2006).

13. It is important to remember that by epistemological disjunctivism we are here considering a particular thesis, and yet potentially there are other views that could fall under this description, more generally conceived. For example, one could image a version of epistemological disjunctivism which holds only that the general epistemic standing of one's belief (as opposed to the specific rational standing) in the non-deceived case is significantly different to the general epistemic standing of one's belief in the parallel deceived case. I don't think such a view by itself entails metaphysical disjunctivism any more than the type of epistemological disjunctivism that concerns us, but even if this were the case it would not be relevant for our purposes. In short, I am not claiming that there is no rendering of the general epistemological disjunctivist idea that entails (a version of) metaphysical disjunctivism, but only that epistemological disjunctivism as we are construing that thesis does not have this entailment.

14. Various commentators have argued that epistemological disjunctivism does not in itself entail metaphysical disjunctivism. See, for example, Snowdon (2005), Millar (2007; 2008), Byrne and Logue (2008), and Pritchard (2008b). In particular, the claim in this regard is often that epistemological disjunctivism

is compatible with a causal theory of perceptual experience, as defended, for example, by Grice (1961) and Strawson (1974). McDowell seems to hold that epistemological disjunctivism is compatible with the denial of metaphysical disjunctivism too. For example, consider this passage:

> The essential thing is that the two sides of the disjunction differ in epistemic significance, whereas on the highest common factor conception the 'good' disjunct can afford no better warrant for perceptual claims than the 'bad' disjunct. This difference in epistemic significance is of course consistent with all sorts of commonalities between the disjuncts. (McDowell 2008, 382n)

For further discussion of the logical connections between metaphysical and epistemological disjunctivism, see Haddock and Macpherson (2008b), Byrne and Logue (2009b), Fish (2009), and Soteriou (2009, esp. §2.4).

15. Note that the entailment thesis is a logically weaker claim than the thesis that seeing that p constitutes a particular way of knowing that p (call this the *way of knowing* thesis). As Cassam (2007b, 339) points out, that one regrets that p is usually thought to entail that one knows that p, and yet regretting that p is obviously not a way of knowing that p. The entailment thesis thus doesn't entail the way of knowing thesis. In contrast, if the way of knowing thesis is true, then it would follow that the entailment thesis is true also, since seeing that p would always go hand-in-hand with knowing that p. (This last entailment might seem obviously true, to the extent that it is not even worth spelling out. But as Cassam (2007b, 339) also demonstrates, it doesn't necessarily follow that a way of knowing that p entails that one knows that p. The example he gives to illustrate this is that of reading that p in an authoritative book. This is clearly a way of knowing that p, but it is compatible with one not knowing that p.) In any case, if we can show that the logically weaker entailment thesis is false, then we will have also shown that the logically stronger way of knowing thesis is false too.

16. Interestingly, McDowell is often credited with the thesis that seeing that p entails believing that p, and yet he explicitly disavows this entailment. For example, Stroud (2002) interprets McDowell's view in this fashion, but in his response to this paper—see McDowell (2002b, 277–8)—McDowell is clear that this is not his position.

17. McDowell agrees. Consider the following passage:

> 'I thought I was looking at your sweater under one of those lights that make it impossible to tell what colours things are, but I now realize I was actually seeing that it was brown.' In saying this, one registers that one had, at the relevant past time, an entitlement that one did not then realize one had. One was in a position to acquire a bit of knowledge

about the world, but because of a misapprehension about the circumstances, one did not avail oneself of the opportunity. (McDowell 2003, 680–81)

I am grateful to Adrian Haddock for alerting me to this passage. See Haddock (2011) for further discussion of McDowell's remarks in this respect.

18. Scott Sturgeon has pointed out to me that there is an interesting analogy here with the point made by Christensen (e.g., 2010) about how higher-order evidence can undermine the excellent evidential support one has for one's first-order beliefs.

19. See, for example, Williamson (2000a, ch. 1). See also Cassam (2007b). For a recent critical discussion of the idea that remembering that *p* entails knowing that *p*, see Bernecker (2007).

20. Since writing this section, John Turri has alerted me to a recent paper of his in which he offers further arguments against what I am here calling the entailment thesis. See Turri (2010).

21. Although I set this complication to one side here, I would be inclined to class an environment which could so very easily have been objectively epistemically problematic, but in fact happens not to be, as objectively epistemically bad, though obviously this is potentially controversial. I am grateful to Adam Carter for pressing me on this point.

22. Notice that this distinction does not categorize as either subjectively good or bad those cases in which the agent is able to neutralize the defeater. Such cases raise complexities of their own which do not concern us here, and so we will simply be setting them to one side in what follows.

23. Relatedly, we will treat any case in which an agent merely *thinks* that she has grounds to doubt the target proposition (but in fact doesn't) as also subjectively epistemically bad.

24. It is a commonplace in epistemology that knowledge requires non-lucky cognitive success—or, as I express the point in Pritchard (2005a, ch. 6), that knowledge is incompatible with 'veritic epistemic luck'—and as such I won't be exploring it further here. I examine this claim about knowledge at length in a number of places. See, for example, Pritchard (2005a; 2007a; 2008c; 2012a; cf. Haddock, Pritchard, and Millar 2010, ch. 3). For a recent critical exchange on this issue, see Hetherington (2013) and Pritchard (2013).

25. The example used here to illustrate a merely bad case is essentially the famous 'barn façade' example described by Goldman (1976), who in turn credits it to Carl Ginet. While most epistemologists grant that knowledge is lacking in this case—on account of the lucky cognitive success in play (see endnote 24 above)—there has been some dissent on this issue. See, especially, Sosa (2007, ch. 5; cf. Gendler and Hawthorne 2005). I critically discuss Sosa's reasons for ascribing knowledge in this case in Pritchard (2009a; 2012a). In

any case, note that any Gettier-style case involving perceptual belief would have sufficed as an illustration of a merely bad scenario, and thus it is not particularly important that a barn façade case be invoked. For example, the famous case offered by Chisholm (1977, 105) of the farmer who truly believes that there is a sheep in the field because he sees a sheep-shaped object (which is not a sheep) would also fit this template. The only difference is that in Chisholm's example the agent does not even see a sheep, while the agent in the barn façade case does at least see a barn (even while failing to see that there is a barn).

26. For more on the epistemological disjunctivist response to the basis problem, see Pritchard (2011*a*).

27. If one is convinced by epistemological disjunctivism, then one might be tempted to suppose that even this piece of conventional wisdom is false, on the ground that Gettier-style cases effectively presuppose that one's knowledge-adequate rational basis for belief is always non-factive (something that of course epistemological disjunctivism denies). This is an issue that I will not be pursuing here, however, since it will take us too far afield given that our focus is just on the rational basis available in the specific case of paradigmatic perceptual knowledge (and not on the rational basis of our knowledge in general).

28. I talk here of a 'substantive' internal epistemic condition because there may be very weak internal epistemic conditions that even the epistemic externalist might think are necessary for knowledge, such as a 'no defeater' condition. See, for example, Goldman (1979). For a helpful recent discussion of the role of no-defeater conditions in epistemic externalist theories, see Greco (2010, ch. 10).

29. The *locus classicus* for defences of process reliabilism is Goldman (1979; cf. Goldman 1986).

30. For a key defence of accessibilism, see Chisholm (1977). See also, BonJour (1985, ch. 2). For some helpful recent discussions of accessibilism and its role in the wider epistemological externalism/internalism debate, see Steup (1999), Pryor (2001, §3), BonJour (2002), Pappas (2005), and Poston (2008).

31. The *locus classicus* for defences of mentalism is Conee and Feldman (2004). For a set of critical discussions of this proposal, see Dougherty (2011). I discuss this view in the context of epistemological disjunctivism in Pritchard (2011*b*), to which Conee and Feldman (2011) is a response.

32. Until recently, I think that this claim would have struck most epistemologists as very implausible, but Williamson's writings on this topic—see, especially, Williamson (1995; 2000*a*)—have prompted many to rethink their view on this score.

33. More precisely, there is no essential tension between these two views insofar as we confine our attention to paradigm cases of perceptual knowledge. For example, if seeing that p can come apart from knowing that p, as I have argued above, then there is the potential for there to be a clash between epistemological disjunctivism and mentalism. I set this issue to one side here.

34. The *locus classicus* for discussion of the new evil genius thesis is Lehrer and Cohen (1983). See also Cohen (1984). Note, however, that this formulation of the thesis is my own. For an excellent survey of recent work in epistemology on this issue, see Littlejohn (2009).

35. The new evil genius thesis is often presented by epistemic internalists as posing a problem for epistemic externalism—*viz.*, how is this view to account for the fact that intuitively an agent and her recently envatted physical counterpart have beliefs which enjoy a common kind of epistemic support? In response to this problem a number of epistemic externalists have tried to offer ways of accommodating the intuitions that lie behind this thesis. For two influential discussions in this regard, see Goldman (1988) and Sosa (2003, 159–61). See also Bach (1985) and Engel (1992).

36. I think that a failure to clearly distinguish epistemological disjunctivism from other standard epistemic internalist proposals lies at the heart of a general inability amongst contemporary epistemologists to get to grips with the true nature of the epistemological disjunctivist proposal. This is particularly true with regard to McDowell's version of epistemological disjunctivism, which as I explain in the introduction is the inspiration for the view defended here. On the one hand, the fact that rational support on his view can be factive has led some to describe him as an epistemic externalist (e.g., Greco 2004). On the other hand, his avowed epistemic internalism has led others to suppose that his claim that rational support is factive should not be taken at face value (e.g., Brandom 1995; Wright 2002). For a more in-depth discussion of McDowell's view in this regard, see Neta and Pritchard (2007).

37. Recall that in order to keep the discussion simple we are here bracketing the extent to which the presence of defeaters can make some kinds of 'bad' case—e.g., a bad+ case—potentially introspectively distinguishable from the corresponding good+ case. If one prefers, one can simply run the argument with a particular kind of bad case in mind, one that does not involve defeaters.

38. See Goldman (1988) for a very similar response to the new evil genius thesis, albeit one where the argumentative line put forth is from an explicitly reliabilist perspective. Inevitably, such an approach to the problem is regarded in certain quarters as controversial. In particular, it is sometimes suggested that in order to account for the intuitions behind the new evil genius thesis it is not enough to appeal to a broadly 'negative' species of epistemic support such as epistemic blamelessness. Rather, we must further show that our subject and

her recently envatted counterpart possess a significant degree of positive epistemic support in common. See, for example, BonJour (2002). For further discussion of this issue, see Littlejohn (2009, §2). Note also that there are some important issues surrounding the idea of a specifically epistemic conception of blamelessness—and, more generally, the idea of a specifically epistemic deontology—though I will not be exploring these issues here. The *locus classicus* for discussions of epistemic deontology is Alston (1986). See also Pryor (2001, §4) and Adler (2002).

39. Note that if one wished to formulate a general principle to the effect that introspectively indistinguishable cases entail a common degree of epistemic blamelessness on the part of the subjects concerned, then one would need to tread with care. This is because introspective indistinguishability is a binary non-transitive relation, while sameness of degree of epistemic blamelessness is presumably a binary transitive relation. Any such principle would thus be at the mercy of 'Sorites-style' reasoning. One novel option in this regard, suggested to me by Allan Hazlett, would be to employ a relation on the right hand side of the principle which has the same logical properties as the relation that appears on the left hand side of the principle (e.g., to talk of the degree of epistemic blamelessness on the part of the two subjects as not being identical but rather merely indistinguishable).

40. McDowell makes this point himself, arguing that we should not confuse mere epistemic blamelessness with the kind of robust epistemic standings that he credits to agents in good+ cases. Consider, for example, the following passage:

> No doubt some notion of entitlement or justification might have application in [. . . *the bad*] case. It might be rational (doxastically blameless) for the subject—who only seems to see a candle in front of her—to claim that there is a candle in front of her. But this is not the notion of entitlement or justification that should figure in a gloss on the Sellarsian thought that knowledge is a standing in the space of reasons. The right notion for Sellars's point is [. . .] a notion for which entitlement and truth do not come apart. (McDowell 2002a, 99)

41. Notice that the point being made here is not that seeing that *p* in such cases offers no epistemic support for believing that *p*, for this is clearly false. For one thing, as noted above, according to epistemological disjunctivism seeing that *p* necessarily puts one in a good position to know that *p* and so on this view manifestly does offer epistemic support for a belief that *p*. What is key, however, is that if this factive reason is not the reason on which the agent's knowledge is based, then it will not offer *reflectively accessible* epistemic support.

PART TWO

Favouring versus Discriminating Epistemic Support

Introductory Remarks

The aim of part two is to introduce a general distinction between favouring and discriminating epistemic support and show how a failure to pay due attention to this distinction has impaired certain key discussions in contemporary epistemology, in ways that are centrally relevant to epistemological disjunctivism. To this end we will be examining the relationship between perceptual knowledge and discrimination in light of the so-called 'relevant alternatives' intuition.

As a starting point for our discussion we will investigate an intuitive relevant alternatives account of perceptual knowledge which incorporates the insight that there is a close connection between perceptual knowledge and the possession of relevant discriminatory abilities. As we will see, however, in order to resolve certain problems that face this view it is essential to recognize the aforementioned distinction between favouring and discriminating epistemic support. This distinction complicates the story regarding how an alternative becomes relevant, and in doing so weakens the connection between perceptual knowledge and discrimination. The theory that results, however—what I term a 'two-tiered' relevant alternatives theory of perceptual knowledge—accommodates many of our intuitions about perceptual knowledge and so avoids the revisionism of some recent proposals in the epistemological literature.

As we will see at the end of part two, this way of thinking about perceptual knowledge—and, especially, the distinction between favouring and discriminating epistemic support that underlies it—is of particular interest to defenders of epistemological disjunctivism. Indeed, it holds the key to resolving the distinguishability problem that was left standing at the end of part one. The goal of part two is thus twofold. First, to demonstrate that there is an important distinction to be drawn between favouring and discriminating epistemic support, a distinction which all epistemologists (i.e., and not just epistemological disjunctivists) need to take on board. Second, to show that with this distinction in play the epistemological landscape is far more favourable to epistemological disjunctivism than it might at first appear, on account of how the epistemological disjunctivist can employ this distinction to block the distinguishability problem. An independently plausible epistemological distinction is thus shown to lend support to epistemological disjunctivism.

§1. The Relevant Alternatives Account of Perceptual Knowledge

Intuitively, there is a very close connection between perceptual knowledge and discrimination. Looking out of my window, I come to perceptually know that the creature before me is a goldfinch because I can, via perception, discriminate goldfinches from other things that might plausibly be in the neighbourhood (such as woodpeckers, to use J. L. Austin's (1961) example). Of course, in my present situation I can't discriminate between goldfinches and, say, hologram goldfinches, but intuitively this sort of contrast is by-the-by. My knowing that there is a goldfinch in the garden is essentially constituted—at least in major part—by my being able to discriminate between goldfinches and plausible non-goldfinch alternatives; not by my being able to discriminate between goldfinches and *im*plausible non-goldfinch alternatives, such as the 'hologram goldfinch' alternative.[1]

This way of thinking about the relationship between perceptual knowledge and discrimination fits very neatly with an intuition that is widespread in epistemology, what I will refer to as the *core relevant alternatives intuition*. This intuition states that in order to know a proposition, *p*, what is required is that one is able to rule out all those not-*p* alternatives that are (in some sense to be specified) *relevant*. What is not required is that one is able to rule out the *ir*relevant alternatives.

Notice that the conception of perceptual knowledge just described, which treats such knowledge as being essentially concerned with the possession of certain discriminatory capacities, seems to represent one way of fleshing out the core relevant alternatives intuition in the perceptual case. To begin with, it offers an answer to the question of what it means to 'rule out' an alternative. In the perceptual case at least, to be able to rule out an alternative is to be able, via perception, to make the relevant discriminations between the target object and the object at issue in the alternative—e.g., to be able to perceptually discriminate between gold-finches and woodpeckers.

Moreover, we also have an answer to the crucial question of what determines relevance, at least in the perceptual case. For what makes an alternative relevant is whether it is the kind of alternative that might ordinarily obtain in one's neighbourhood. The possibility that one is looking at a woodpecker right now is relevant to one's belief that one is presently looking at a goldfinch because woodpeckers are the kinds of things that one might ordinarily find in one's environment. In contrast, the possibility that one is looking at a hologram goldfinch just now is *not* relevant because this is not the kind of thing that one might ordinarily find in one's environment.

I think the best way of capturing what is going on here is in modal terms by saying that the class of relevant alternatives is, roughly, all those alter-natives that obtain in nearby possible worlds.[2] On this reading of rele-vance, if one had the misfortune to be in an abnormal environment in which there were nearby possible worlds in which what one was looking at just now was not a goldfinch but a hologram goldfinch, then in order to be able to know that what one is looking at is a goldfinch, one would have to be able to perceptually discriminate between goldfinches and hologram goldfinches. In this environment, then, it is very hard to know that one is looking at a goldfinch (in that it would require further inquiries on the part of the agent, such as a much closer examination), even though this is something that is very easy to know in normal environments.

That one's environment can in this way have an impact on how hard it is to acquire perceptual knowledge is perfectly in accordance with intui-tion, as the famous barn façade case illustrates. Gaining perceptual knowl-edge that what one is looking at is a barn in a normal environment is very easy, since it merely demands very mundane discriminatory powers. In contrast, gaining perceptual knowledge that what one is looking at is a barn in an abnormal environment in which barn façades are the norm is very hard, since it demands very specialized discriminatory powers—in particular, it demands the ability to perceptually discriminate between barns and barn façades.

We thus get the following relevant alternatives account of perceptual knowledge:

The Relevant Alternatives Account of Perceptual Knowledge
S has perceptual knowledge that ϕ only if S can perceptually discriminate the target object at issue in ϕ from the objects at issue in relevant alternative (not-ϕ) propositions, where a relevant alternative is an alternative that obtains in a nearby possible world.[3]

This relevant alternatives account of perceptual knowledge leads to a pleasing result. Perceptual knowledge, it turns out, is often very easy to possess. At least in normal environments, I can know relatively mundane perceptual truths simply in virtue of being able to undertake relatively mundane perceptual discriminations.[4] And this seems just right.

§2. Relevant Alternatives and Closure

As Fred Dretske (1970) famously showed, however, there is a problem lying in wait for any relevant alternatives account of perceptual knowledge of this sort; a problem that is brought out by considering the principle that knowledge is closed under competent deductions, or the *closure principle* for short. This principle can be formulated as follows:

> *The Closure Principle*
> If S knows that ϕ, and S competently deduces ψ from ϕ (thereby coming to believe that ψ while retaining her knowledge that ϕ), then S knows that ψ.[5]

So construed, the principle seems utterly uncontentious. The problem posed by this principle for the relevant alternatives account of perceptual knowledge is that we only need to suppose that the agent concerned knows certain entailments, and makes competent deductions on the basis of this knowledge, in order to get a situation in which in order to know a proposition—e.g., that one is presently looking at a goldfinch—one needs to be able to know that certain intuitively far-fetched error-possibilities—e.g., that one is presently looking at a hologram goldfinch—are false.

For example, suppose that one knows that one is looking at a goldfinch right now, and one also knows that if one is looking at a goldfinch right now then one is not looking at a hologram goldfinch, and one makes a competent deduction on this basis. It follows, given the closure principle, that one knows that one is not now looking at a hologram goldfinch, and thus knowing that one is looking at a goldfinch in this case entails knowing in addition that one is not looking at a hologram goldfinch. In effect, then, knowing that one is looking at a goldfinch in this case entails knowing that one is looking at a goldfinch *rather than* a hologram goldfinch. The trouble is, of course, that one is unable to perceptually discriminate between goldfinches and hologram goldfinches—it is not as if one has made any special checks in this regard, for example—and yet it now seems that it is incumbent upon one to be able to rule out this possibility—i.e., know it to be false—in order to know something so mundane as that one is presently looking at a goldfinch. Perceptual knowledge of mundane truths can thus sometimes be very difficult to come by, even in normal environments. The key advantage of the relevant alternatives account of perceptual knowledge—that it can account for how perceptual knowledge can be quite easy to acquire in normal environments—therefore appears to be under threat.

Famously, Dretske concluded on this basis that the closure principle should be abandoned. If we stick to the core relevant alternatives intuition, argues Dretske, then we should insist that knowing that one is looking at, say, a goldfinch should never (in normal circumstances anyway) require the ability to rule out the irrelevant 'hologram goldfinch' alternative. Since accepting the closure principle would require one in certain cases to rule out (i.e., know to be false) these irrelevant hypotheses, thereby making perceptual knowledge very hard to come by, then this principle has to go, at least if scepticism is to be avoided.

The example that Dretske used to illustrate this point was the famous 'zebra' case. Imagine a person—we'll call her 'Zula'—who is at the zoo, and who gets a good look at one of the zebras in the clearly marked zebra enclosure. Zula has all the usual cognitive abilities and background knowledge one would expect of a normal person, and the circumstances are in every relevant respect entirely normal too. Does Zula know that what she is looking at is a zebra? Intuitively, we would say so. Her belief meets many of the criteria we might wish to lay down on a theory of knowledge. For example, it is reliably formed, it is virtuously formed, it is safe (i.e., roughly, her true belief could not have easily been false), it is sensitive (i.e., roughly, had what she believed been false, then she wouldn't have believed it), it is evidentially well-founded, and so on.

The trouble is, we can stipulate that Zula happens to know that if what she is looking at is a zebra, then it follows that what she is looking at is not a cleverly disguised mule, and that she makes a competent deduction on this basis. Given the closure principle, it therefore follows that Zula knows that she is not looking at a cleverly disguised mule, and thus that she knows that what she is looking at is a zebra *rather than* a cleverly disguised mule. The problem, however, is that Zula is just a normal person with normal epistemic powers. Accordingly, she's in no position to perceptually discriminate between zebras and cleverly disguised mules. It is not as if she has some special expertise in this regard—such as might be possessed by a zoologist, for example—or that she has made any special checks—such as going up to the creature and checking for paint. Thus, the closure principle seems to require that in order for Zula to know that she is looking at a zebra she must be able to rule out (i.e., know to be false) the cleverly disguised mule hypothesis. But since Zula lacks the discriminative abilities to do this, we have a problem. As with the goldfinch case described earlier, there is a tension between the core relevant alternatives intuition (as it is applied to perceptual knowledge) and the closure principle, and in light of this tension Dretske's recommendation is to abandon the closure principle.[6]

Denying the closure principle is not an easy thing to do, however, since the principle is so incredibly compelling. Moreover, I think there has been a general consensus that the kind of epistemology that Dretske and others have advanced (e.g., Nozick 1981) in order to account for the failure of the closure principle brings with it some fairly serious problems. What is common to these views is a commitment to something like the sensitivity principle as a condition on knowledge: roughly, that one's belief should be such that, had what one believed not been true, one would not have believed it. One key problem that faces such proposals is that once the sensitivity principle is expressed in the right way, then it is no longer obvious that it generates the kinds of counterexamples to the closure principle that it was designed to explain, and nor is it obvious that it is authentic to the core relevant alternatives intuition that motivated the rejection of this principle in the first place.[7]

Although few these days are inclined to deny the closure principle, there is a new proposal on the scene which does something very similar. This position is known as *contrastivism*, and has been defended by Jonathan Schaffer (2005), amongst others.[8] According to the contrastivist, knowledge is to be always understood contrastively, in the sense that one never knows that *p simpliciter*. Instead, one knows that *p* rather than each one of a set of contrasts (i.e., alternatives) to *p*, where knowing that a proposition obtains rather than one of the contrasts is explicitly understood in terms of discriminating the target proposition from the specified contrasts. So, for example, on this view Zula knows that what she is looking at is a zebra rather than an undisguised horse or baboon, because she can make the relevant perceptual discriminations. But Zula doesn't know that what she is looking at is a zebra rather than a cleverly disguised mule, because in this case she cannot make the relevant perceptual discriminations. Crucially, though, there is no sense to the idea that Zula either does or does not know that what she is looking at is a zebra where this is not qualified to a contrast set.

Although contrastivists would claim that they do not deny the closure principle—they would argue that they can retain a 'contrastivized' version of this principle, though I am somewhat sceptical about this—they do (at least) deny that there is any sense in which Zula knows that what she is looking at is not a cleverly disguised mule, and in this regard their view is in the same revisionistic spirit as Dretske's non-closure view.[9]

There is also a second, and I think more important, sense in which the contrastivist view and the Dretskean view are closely connected. This concerns the fact that they both regard what it takes to rule out an alternative as ultimately being a discriminative capacity. For the contrastivist, this point is explicit to the view. To rule out an alternative to what one knows is to know that the target proposition obtains rather than the alternative, where knowing that one proposition obtains rather than an alternative is in turn understood in terms of the possession of the relevant discriminatory capacity. For the Dretskean, this point is a little more implicit to the view. To rule out an alternative to what one knows by the lights of this proposal is to know that the target proposition is true and that the (known) alternative is false. Crucially, however, it is clear that Dretske holds that, at least in the perceptual case, knowing that the target proposition obtains rather than a known alternative entails that one can perceptually discriminate between the object at issue in the target proposition and the object at issue in the alternative. It is only if Dretske holds this further thesis that it follows from the fact that Zula lacks the relevant discriminatory abilities (but knows that the creature before her is a zebra nonetheless) that the closure principle must fail. (We will come back to this point in a moment.)

It is not peculiar to the Dretskean and contrastivist views that they ultimately understand what it is to rule out an alternative in terms of discriminatory abilities. After all, this sort of account of what it takes to rule out an alternative is implicit in the intuitive picture of perceptual knowledge that we noted in §1 above, a picture on which there is a very tight connection between possessing perceptual knowledge and possessing the relevant discriminatory abilities. I suggest, however, that this conception of what it takes to rule out an alternative—and the picture of the relationship between perceptual knowledge and perceptual discrimination that goes hand-in-hand with it, including the relevant alternatives account of perceptual knowledge that this picture gives rise to—is not quite right. In particular, I will be arguing that there is a sense in which one can rule out an alternative where this is not to be construed in terms of a discriminative ability. As we will see, this point has a number of important ramifications for our understanding of knowledge, and perceptual knowledge in particular.

§3. Three Epistemic Principles: Discrimination, Evidential Transmission, and Favouring

Let us look again at the problem that Dretske thought was posed by the closure principle. We have already noted that it is essential to the setting-up of this problem that we take for granted the kind of epistemological picture of the relationship between perceptual knowledge and perceptual discrimination that was sketched above in §1. It is worthwhile spelling this point out in more detail.

Consider the following plausible principle:

The Discrimination Principle
If S has perceptual knowledge that ϕ, and S knows that another (known to be inconsistent) alternative ψ does not obtain, then S must be able to perceptually discriminate between the object at issue in ϕ and the object at issue in ψ.[10]

So, for example, if Zula knows that what she is looking at is a zebra, and she also knows that what she is looking at is not a cleverly disguised mule (bearing in mind that she knows the relevant entailment)—i.e., if she knows that what she is looking at is a zebra *rather than* a cleverly disguised mule—then she must be able to perceptually discriminate between zebras and cleverly disguised mules.

Dretske certainly seems to be buying into a principle of this sort, since it is only with this principle in play that it follows immediately from the closure principle that there is a problem in the zebra case. That is, it is only if we construe the fact that Zula is able to know that what she is looking at is a zebra rather than a cleverly disguised mule as entailing a capacity to perceptually discriminate between zebras and cleverly disguised mules—something which, *ex hypothesi*, she is unable to do—that we get a straightforward contradiction. Without this principle, all that follows is that Zula is, it seems, able to know that one proposition has obtained rather than an alternative even while being unable to perceptually discriminate between the object at issue in the target proposition and the object at issue in the alternative. This in itself is mysterious, especially when we are dealing with perceptual knowledge, but it is not yet contradictory.[11]

Suppose that we took it for granted that the closure principle should be endorsed. We might thus regard the discrimination principle as suspect, despite its initial plausibility. The goal would then be to find a suitable explanation for the failure of the discrimination principle while also accounting for the mysterious nature of Zula's knowledge: how could it be that she knows that what she is looking at is a zebra rather than a cleverly disguised mule, given that she is unable to perceptually discriminate between zebras and cleverly disguised mules?

One way of responding to this problem could be to argue for the rejection of the discrimination principle on anti-luck grounds. After all, given Zula's epistemic position (in particular, that she knows that what she is looking at is a zebra, and that if it is a zebra then it is not a cleverly disguised mule), it is not a matter of *luck* that Zula's belief that she is not looking at a cleverly disguised mule is true. Her belief could not, for example, have very easily been false. So if knowledge is essentially non-lucky true belief, as some have argued, then there is *something* that can be said in favour of the idea that Zula has knowledge of this deduced proposition, even though she is unable to perceptually discriminate between zebras and cleverly disguised mules.[12]

Still, the nagging worry remains that it is odd that Zula is able to know such a thing given that she lacks the relevant discriminatory capacities. Indeed, even if we set aside this problem which is posed by the discrimination principle, there appears to be a further difficulty which faces the idea that Zula can know the deduced proposition. This aspect of the problem concerns the *evidential* status of Zula's putative knowledge in this respect. In particular, the closure principle forces us to regard Zula as knowing that what she is looking at is not a cleverly disguised mule, and yet she doesn't appear to have any good supporting evidence for this knowledge. Moreover, although we might not claim that all knowledge must be evidentially grounded, all will surely agree that knowledge of a proposition like this must be so grounded. Call this the *evidential problem*.

There are two ways of bringing this evidential problem into sharp relief. Perhaps the most immediate way to do this is by appealing to a specifically evidential version of the so-called 'transmission principle', which many have distinguished from the closure principle. Consider the following *evidential transmission principle*:

> The Evidential Transmission Principle
> If S perceptually knows that ϕ in virtue of evidence set E, and S competently deduces ψ from ϕ (thereby coming to believe that ψ while retaining her knowledge that ϕ), then S knows that ψ where that knowledge is sufficiently supported by E.[13]

This principle certainly does seem compelling, at least insofar as we restrict our attention to those propositions which, if known at all, are known in virtue of appropriate supporting evidence. How could it be that you have sufficient supporting evidence for perceptual knowledge of one proposition, and then undertake a competent deduction, and yet fail to have sufficient evidence to support knowledge of the second proposition? For example, if a detective knows, in virtue of her evidence, that such-and-such is the (sole) murderer of the victim, and she competently deduces on this basis that another person (a previous suspect, say) is not the murderer, then how could it be that she lacks an adequate evidential basis for knowledge of the entailed proposition?

The problem is, of course, that when applied to the zebra case this principle entails that the evidence that Zula has in support of her knowledge that what she is looking at is a zebra ought to be sufficient to support her knowledge that what she is looking at is not a cleverly disguised mule. What is odd about this is that Zula's evidence for thinking that what she is looking at is a zebra does not seem to speak at all to the cleverly disguised mule alternative. As we noted above, it is not as if Zula has any special expertise in this regard—such as might be possessed by a zoologist, for example—nor has Zula made any special checks. It is thus mysterious how her evidence could transfer across the deduction. One who wishes to retain the closure principle thus seems committed to denying not just the discrimination principle, but also the evidential transmission principle.

The second way to bring the evidential problem into sharp relief—indeed, a way of bringing the problem into sharp relief that gets more to the heart of the matter I think—is by appeal to what is known as the 'favouring principle'.[14] We can formulate this principle as follows, where 'better' evidence is evidence that makes the target proposition more likely to be true:

The Favouring Principle
If S (i) knows that ϕ, and (ii) knows that ψ, and (iii) knows that ϕ entails ψ, then S has better evidence in support of her belief that ϕ than for believing that not-ψ.

As with the evidential transmission principle, this principle certainly seems compelling, at least as regards those propositions which, if known at all, one knows in virtue of possessing appropriate supporting evidence. How can it be that one knows that one proposition obtains and that a second, known to incompatible, alternative does not obtain, and yet one lacks better evidence for believing the first proposition rather than believing the alternative? Put more simply, how can one know that one alternative obtains rather than a second alternative, when one lacks better evidence for thinking that the first alternative obtains rather than the second?

Applied to the zebra case, however, this principle entails that if Zula knows that what she is looking at is a zebra, and also knows that what she is looking at is not a cleverly disguised mule (and the relevant entailment), then she must have better evidence for believing that what she is looking at is a zebra than for believing that what she is looking at is a cleverly disguised mule. Such a demand seems entirely reasonable, but the prob-lem, of course, is that intuitively Zula lacks such 'favouring' evidence in support of her belief. Intuitively, that is, since her evidence does not speak to the cleverly disguised mule alternative it can hardly be thought to favour her believing that what she is looking at is a zebra over her believing the alternative that what she is looking at is a cleverly disguised mule. Anyone retaining the closure principle in the zebra case therefore seems to be required to deny the favouring principle as well. The problems facing any view which retains the closure principle thus seem to be mounting up.

So if we wish to retain the closure principle, then there is a burden upon us to explain what this knowledge of the entailed proposition is in virtue of, and that means that we both need to account for the failure of the discrimination principle whilst also responding to this evidential challenge posed by the evidential transmission and favouring principles. I think that the key to resolving both these problems is to recognize that Zula's evidential position is in fact much stronger than we ordinarily tend to think, and certainly strong enough to satisfy the requirements laid down by the evidential transmission and favouring principles.[15]

§4. Favouring and Discriminating Epistemic Support

Consider again the evidential support that Zula has for her knowledge that what she is looking at is a zebra. Now one might naturally say that Zula's knowledge of this proposition is knowledge that she has gained just by looking, and this way of speaking implies that the only evidence that Zula has in favour of her belief is the evidence she gets just by looking—i.e., evidence regarding the visual scene before her. If this is all the evidence that Zula has for her belief—and granting that she has knowledge of the relevant entailment—then it ought to be clear that her knowledge of this proposition fails to satisfy the favouring principle, since the evidence that she gains just by looking in no way favours the 'zebra' alternative over the 'cleverly disguised mule' alternative. And if it fails to satisfy the favouring principle, then how can it satisfy the evidential transmission principle?

I'm actually somewhat suspicious of the idea that Zula can come to know that what she is looking at is a zebra 'just by looking', at least if this phrase is meant to indicate that the evidential support that Zula has for her belief is merely that evidence which is offered by the bare visual scene before her. That is, I think that while there is a sense in which it is obviously true that Zula gains her knowledge just by looking—in that Zula does nothing more than look in order to gain her knowledge—one can grant this straightforward reading of this locution while objecting to the evidential conclusion that is drawn from it. After all, perceptual knowledge can at least sometimes—and perhaps often, or even always—involve a wide range of specialist expertise and background knowledge. Without such expertise and background knowledge, one may look all one wants and still come to know nothing of consequence. But given that such expertise and background knowledge would surely have ramifications for the total evidence that you possess in support of your belief, it follows that coming to know a proposition just by looking need not entail that the only evidence you possess for your belief is the evidence you gained from the bare visual scene before you.

We will set this concern to one side, however, since even if one grants that someone can come to know a proposition on the basis of evidence gained merely by looking in this restrictive sense, it still remains that there is a problem with the standard way of understanding the evidential basis of Zula's belief that what she is looking at is a zebra. Let us grant, then, that Zula's belief in this proposition is adequately supported by the evidence she gains from the bare visual scene presented to her, no matter what further evidence she might possess in favour of this belief. Keeping this set of evidence fixed, and now imagining Zula becoming aware of the relevant entailment and making a competent deduction on this basis, we are faced with the question of how Zula's evidence, so construed, could in any way be good evidence for believing the deduced proposition. How can the evidence Zula gains just by looking in this case have any bearing on the possibility that what she is looking at is a cleverly disguised mule? More pertinently, how can the evidence that she gains in this way supply her with better reason to believe that what she is looking at is a zebra rather than a cleverly disguised mule, as the favouring principle would demand? Moreover, how can the evidence which she gains in this way supply her with knowledge-supporting evidence in favour of her deduced belief that she is not looking at a cleverly disguised mule, as the evidential transmission principle would demand?

Notice, however, that in the setting-up of this problem a key issue is being glossed over, which is what epistemic effect Zula's becoming aware of the entailment has. It is surely right to suppose that Zula can come to know that what she is looking at is a zebra without having any awareness of the cleverly disguised mule hypothesis. But is it really so plausible that Zula can become aware of this error-possibility and its incompatibility with what she believes, *and* retain her knowledge that what she is looking at is a zebra, even while taking no view at all regarding what would entitle her to dismiss such an error-possibility?

In order to see the implausibility of this suggestion, put yourself into Zula's shoes for a moment. Surely in becoming aware of this error-possibility and its incompatibility with what you believe, you would form a view about what entitles you to dismiss this possibility (assuming, of course, that you retain your original belief, and so think that you should dismiss this possibility)? Moreover, I take it that there is quite a lot of evidence that you could offer in favour of taking this view. Think, for example, of the wealth of background knowledge that you have which is relevant to this error-possibility—in particular, evidence regarding the likelihood of this error-possibility obtaining. One might reason, for instance, that there would be no point to such a deception, that it would be costly and time-consuming without bringing any comparable benefit, that it would be easily found out, and then the zoo-owner would be subject to penalties, and so on. What is important about this process of taking a view about one's entitlement to dismiss this error-possibility is that in engaging in this process one thereby highlights that one has better evidence for believing that one is presently looking at a zebra than for the alternative that one is looking at a cleverly disguised mule.

The favouring principle is thus met in this case, because one *does* have better evidence for believing that what one is looking at is a zebra rather than a cleverly disguised mule. Moreover, since such favouring evidence is possessed there is surely no problem with supposing that the evidential transmission principle is met as well. The point is that in order to undertake the competent deduction at issue in the evidential transmission principle—which, recall, is a competent deduction which preserves the agent's knowledge of the antecedent proposition—it is essential that the agent's evidence set incorporates the favouring evidence that the agent has for preferring the 'zebra' alternative over the 'cleverly disguised mule' alternative. But if the agent has supporting evidence of *this* sort, then it is no longer mysterious that she has evidentially supported knowledge of the deduced proposition.

Of course, it is always possible that Zula lacks the kind of background knowledge at issue here, and so has no good reason to dismiss this error-possibility. But notice that if this is the case then it is no longer plausible to suppose that she retains her knowledge of the target proposition. After all, it is one thing to grant that Zula can have knowledge of this proposition while having no awareness of this error-possibility, and quite another to suppose that she retains this knowledge even while being aware of this error-possibility and being unable to rationally dismiss it. That is, becoming aware of an error-possibility that you know is incompatible with what you believe and being unable to rationally dismiss it is, I would claim, knowledge-defeating.[16]

This is a good point to review where we are. To begin with, we have argued that insofar as Zula retains her perceptual knowledge that what she is looking at is a zebra, then it must be the case that she is in a position to rationally dismiss the cleverly disguised mule error-possibility once she becomes aware of it. Crucially, however, we have also seen that it is perfectly consistent with the idea that Zula is unable to perceptually discriminate between zebras and cleverly disguised mules that she is nevertheless in possession of evidence which would enable her to rationally dismiss this error-possibility, thereby satisfying both the favouring principle and the evidential transmission principle. In such a case, her belief that what she is looking at is not a cleverly disguised mule is appropriately evidentially grounded after all, even though Zula cannot make the relevant perceptual discrimination. The upshot of this is that one can indeed have *bona fide* evidentially supported knowledge that one alternative has obtained rather than another (known to be incompatible) alternative, without this requiring that one has the relevant discriminative capacity. The discrimination principle is thus too strong, and must be rejected.

Moreover, notice that we have achieved this result while appealing to our ordinary intuitive conception of evidence. This result is therefore not hostage to a contentious account of evidence. In particular, at no point in this reasoning have we appealed to a factive conception of evidential support of the kind that would be relevant to epistemological disjunctivism. The point being made here should thus be acceptable to all parties in epistemology.

A distinction has therefore opened up between the kind of epistemic support provided by favouring evidence, and the kind of epistemic support provided by discriminatory capacities, since we have seen that one can have knowledge-supporting favouring evidence even while lacking the relevant discriminatory capacities. In failing to recognize this distinction, the participants in this debate have unduly limited their dialectical options. It is perfectly compatible with the idea that Zula cannot perceptually discriminate between zebras and cleverly disguised mules that she nevertheless has the relevant knowledge-supporting evidence for her beliefs so as to satisfy the favouring and transmission principles. One can thus accept, in line with the closure principle, that Zula can come to know that she is not looking at a cleverly disguised mule without thereby becoming puzzled, given Zula's limited discriminatory capacities, as to how such knowledge is possible.[17] As we will see below, although this is a conclusion which I claim all epistemologists should accept, it will be of particular interest to epistemological disjunctivists, since it enables them to resolve the distinguishability problem.

§5. Diagnosis

A question that one might naturally ask at this point is why this distinction between favouring and discriminating epistemic support has not been widely recognized, especially given that I claim that it is rooted in our everyday conception of the epistemological landscape (and so is not hostage to a specific view of evidence). I think that there are several explanations for this. One explanation concerns the point noted above that when we think about the zebra case we tend to naturally describe Zula's knowledge as knowledge that is gained 'just by looking'. In doing so, we have a tendency to ignore the background knowledge that can be relevant to the evidential support that an agent has for her perceptual knowledge, even in cases where the belief formed is fairly mundane.

Interestingly, even when commentators do consider the wider evidential standing of Zula's belief they still understand such evidence in an unduly restrictive way. For example, in his discussion of Zula's epistemic position, Dretske (1970, 1016) asks whether Zula has examined 'the animals closely enough to detect such a fraud', and it is clear from the ensuing remarks that he thinks that a negative answer to this question has a fairly decisive implication for whether or not we should ascribe knowledge to Zula. Such grounds would indeed be very useful for Zula to have in this regard, but the lack of them does not indicate a lack of knowledge since, as we have seen, it remains that Zula may have adequate favouring evidence in support of her beliefs. Notice that what is happening here is that the kind of additional evidence which Dretske is admitting as relevant is only that *discriminating evidence* which suggests that Zula is able to make the relevant perceptual discrimination (since if she had made such special checks, then she would have been in a position to perceptually discriminate between a zebra and a cleverly disguised mule in this case). One can have the relevant favouring evidence, however, even while lacking such discriminating evidence.

Many commentators have followed Dretske is treating Zula's evidence in this way. Consider the following passage from a paper by Crispin Wright:

You go to the zoo, see several zebras in a pen, and opine (ZEBRA): that those animals are zebras. Well, you know what zebras look like, and these animals look just like that. Surely you are fully warranted in your belief. But if the animals are zebras, then it follows that they are not mules painstakingly and skilfully disguised as zebras. Does your warrant transmit to the latter claim? Did you examine the animals closely enough to detect such a fraud? Almost certainly not. The grounds you have for (ZEBRA)—essentially, just the look of the beasts—have no bearing on this possibility. (Wright 2003a, 60)

Like Dretske, Wright also assumes that the only additional evidence that would be relevant would be discriminating evidence, thereby ignoring the possibility of favouring evidence. In doing so he offers an account of this case in which the agent concerned has knowledge of the target proposition and yet has an epistemic position which fails to satisfy either the favouring or evidential transmission principles. More-over, notice that Wright in addition tends to identify the evidential support that the agent has for her belief with merely the evidence she gains from the bare visual scene presented to her—her evidence is, 'essentially, just the look of the beasts'—when, as we have seen, this is also an unduly restrictive way of understanding the agent's evidential standing. While we have granted for the sake of argument that Zula might well have knowledge that what she is looking at is a zebra merely on this bare evidential basis, it does not follow that Zula can retain this knowledge merely on this basis once she becomes aware of certain error-possibilities.

A further reason why commentators have tended to overlook this distinction between favouring epistemic support and discriminating epi-stemic support is that, at least typically, when one explicitly claims to (perceptually) know a proposition one thereby represents oneself as pos-sessing discriminating evidence in support of that claim rather than just favouring evidence. For example, if Zula were to flatly (i.e., without qualification) claim to know that the creature before her is a zebra in a conversational context in which the cleverly disguised mule error-possibility is at issue, then we would surely regard her as implying that she has discrimi-nating evidence in favour of her belief, such as that she has some special expertise or knowledge in this regard (that she's made special checks, say). If she is unable to do this, then we would expect her to indicate this fact. She might qualify her claim to know, for example, by specifying that the only grounds she has in support of her assertion are favouring grounds (i.e., by citing some of those favouring grounds).

It is an interesting question just why appropriate (unqualified) claims to know typically generate this sort of implicature, and we will be returning to consider this issue further below in part three (see §8). What is important about this observation, however, is that it highlights one reason why one might naturally focus on whether Zula has discriminatory epistemic support when considering her epistemic standing, to the exclusion of other types of epistemic support, especially favouring epistemic support.[18]

One final reason why I think the distinction between favouring and discriminating epistemic support is often overlooked when it comes to these cases is that discussion of zebra-style examples usually takes place with one eye on the problem of radical scepticism. On the face of it, this might seem entirely understandable, since the sceptical challenge—as it is usually formulated at any rate—does seem to be a type of zebra-style case.

For example, suppose that one has perceptual knowledge that one has hands. Suppose further that one knows that if one has hands then one is not a (handless) brain-in-a-vat (BIV) who is undetectably being 'fed' one's experiences by supercomputers, and one undertakes a competent deduction on this basis. Given the closure principle, then, one knows that one is not a BIV. But how can that be, given that, *ex hypothesi*, one cannot perceptually discriminate between having hands and being a BIV? Moreover, the evidential transmission principle and the favouring principle both seem to fail in this case—intuitively, one does not have better evidence for believing that one has hands than for the BIV hypothesis, and neither does the putatively knowledge-supporting evidence one has for believing that one has hands seem to transfer across a competent deduction to be knowledge-supporting evidence for believing that one is not a BIV.

It is best, however, to keep the issue posed by the zebra case and that posed by radical sceptical hypotheses separate, for on closer analysis radical sceptical hypotheses can be shown to pose a far trickier challenge. In particular, a crucial disanalogy between the zebra case and radical sceptical hypotheses is that the latter by their nature call one's evidence into question *en masse*. The BIV hypothesis, for example, is explicitly designed to call into question the evidence one takes oneself to have for thinking that one has hands. In contrast, the truth of the cleverly disguised mule hypothesis has, on the face of it anyway, very little bearing on the strength of Zula's evidence that what she is looking at is a zebra. I think this distinctive feature of sceptical cases ensures that one cannot simply make use of the distinction between favouring and discriminating epistemic support in order to respond to the sceptical case, since it is moot whether one should allow the usual scope of evidence that one would typically ascribe to an agent in light of a sceptical challenge.

For example, just as we appealed to Zula's background knowledge about the plausibility of the cleverly disguised mule hypothesis in order to accord her with the appropriate favouring evidence in support of her beliefs, suppose we appealed to similar background knowledge that our agent in the radical sceptical case might be thought to have in order to accord her with the requisite favouring evidence. After all, we might naturally suppose that the agent in the sceptical case possesses all sorts of good reasons for thinking that the BIV hypothesis is implausible (e.g., that this scenario is incompatible with the current state of technology, that it is not plausible that someone would have a motive to pursue such 'envatments', and so on).

The problem, however, should now be manifest. We can unproblematically appeal to such background knowledge in the case of Zula precisely because the error-possibility at issue does not call into question this background knowledge. The same is not true when we focus on the radical sceptical hypothesis. For if the agent were indeed a BIV, then she would lack such background knowledge. Accordingly, it would be contentious to appeal to such evidence as a means of showing that this agent's beliefs have the required epistemic support. Given this crucial disanalogy between zebra-style cases and radical sceptical cases, having the problem of radical scepticism in the background can thus tend to make the evidential problem posed by zebra-style cases look more intractable than it in fact is.

Note that this is not to say that there is no scope for extending our treatment of the zebra-style cases to the problem of radical scepticism. The point is rather that any such extension of the strategy would require further argumentation. We will be returning to the specific problem posed by radical scepticism in part three. As we will see there, the distinction between favouring and discriminating epistemic support *can* help us resolve the problem of radical scepticism, but only once this distinction is properly embedded within a wider anti-sceptical strategy that incorporates epistemological disjunctivism.

§6. A Two-Tiered Relevant Alternatives Theory

In any case, the state-of-play is that we have identified an important distinction between favouring and discriminating epistemic support, a distinction that can enable us to explain why the discrimination principle should fail while also accounting for the evidential basis of Zula's knowledge that what she is looking at is not a cleverly disguised mule. One might ask where this leaves the relevant alternatives account of perceptual knowledge that we began with.

Recall that this account of perceptual knowledge held that perceptual knowledge is essentially constituted in terms of the possession of those perceptual capacities necessary to discriminate between the object at issue in the target proposition and the objects at issue in the relevant alternatives, where the relevance of an alternative is in turn determined by one's environment. It should be clear from the foregoing that we cannot maintain this conception of perceptual knowledge in its current form, since we have accepted that it is a consequence of the closure principle that in order to have perceptual knowledge of a proposition it is sometimes necessary to possess not just the discriminatory capacities just described, but also relevant favouring evidence. Although this conclusion means that we need to reject the relevant alternatives account of perceptual knowledge as it presently stands, I think we can nevertheless retain the spirit of the view. In particular, I suggest that what we need to do is replace the relevant alternatives account of perceptual knowledge with a two-tiered view that is cast along the same lines.

To begin with, we need to distinguish between a narrow and a broad conception of relevance. The narrow conception of relevance is simply that notion at issue in the relevant alternatives account of perceptual knowledge which concerns those error-possibilities that obtain in nearby possible worlds. One thing that is absolutely right about the relevant alternatives theory of perceptual knowledge is that when it comes to alternatives which are narrowly relevant the possession of the relevant discriminatory capacity *is* essential for knowledge. So if Zula is indeed in an environment in which she could very easily be looking at a cleverly disguised mule just now, then in order to know that the creature before her is a zebra she must be able to perceptually discriminate between zebras and cleverly disguised mules. Since she cannot do this, in this environment she lacks knowledge that what she is looking at is a zebra. But that is, I would argue, entirely what we would expect.

Thus far, then, I am agreeing with Dretske and many others who follow Dretske in holding that there is a very tight connection between perceptual knowledge and perceptual discrimination. We diverge when it comes to those non-narrow alternatives which are also, I would claim, relevant. These are alternatives which are not narrowly relevant in the sense just specified, but which are made relevant by other considerations. One way in which this can happen—and there may be other ways, though I won't be taking a stand on this issue here—is when one becomes aware of an error-possibility which is incompatible with something which one believes. I have argued that if one is to retain one's knowledge of the original proposition, then one must be able to rule out this error-possibility.

On the face of it, admitting this much would seem to entail that in order to have perceptual knowledge of quite mundane propositions, such as that the creature before one is a zebra, one has to know the denials of some quite extraordinary error-possibilities, such as that the creature before one is not a cleverly disguised mule. Accordingly, one might think that perceptual knowledge of quite mundane propositions becomes unduly difficult, and therefore doubt the epistemology that lies behind this demand. As we have seen, however, the epistemic demands made by this requirement are actually quite modest, since all one needs to satisfy it is favouring supporting evidence, and this is usually quite easy to come by, at least if one is reasonably intellectually sophisticated.

In particular, what awareness of these non-narrowly relevant alternatives does not demand, crucially, is the ability to perceptually discriminate between the object at issue in the target proposition and the objects at issue in the non-narrowly relevant alternatives. This epistemic demand would indeed be hard to satisfy, and as such it would make perceptual knowledge of the relatively mundane unduly difficult to acquire. Fortunately, we have seen that the epistemic demand in play when it comes to ruling out non-narrowly relevant alternatives is of the weaker favouring variety rather than the stronger discriminating variety. And since one can usually straightforwardly satisfy this requirement, then accepting such epistemic principles as closure, favouring, and evidential transmission no longer poses a problem because in accepting them one is not obliged to thereby accept that perceptual knowledge of the relatively mundane can sometimes entail quite extraordinary discriminatory powers that one is unlikely to possess.

We thus get a two-tiered picture of relevance which is very much in accord with commonsense. For one thing, it conforms to our intuitive picture of the relationship between perceptual knowledge and perceptual discrimination that we began with, since there *is* still a very close relationship between these two notions in play here. Indeed, in cases in which no non-narrowly relevant alternatives are in play, one can count as having perceptual knowledge purely in virtue of being able to undertake the relevant perceptual discriminations (e.g., one can count as perceptually knowing that the object before one is a goldfinch in virtue of being able to tell goldfinches apart from such items—depending on one's environment—as woodpeckers, or greenfinches).

Moreover, this two-tiered picture of relevance also conforms to the basic thought that underlies the core relevant alternatives intuition, which is that one can have knowledge without having to rule out far-fetched error-possibilities. This is still true. For example, if one is unaware of the non-narrow alternatives—and such alternatives are not made non-narrowly relevant in some other way—then one can know that what one is looking at is a goldfinch without having to rule out the non-narrow, and far-fetched, error-possibility that what one is looking at is, say, a hologram goldfinch.

This two-tiered relevant alternatives theory also accommodates the thought that alternatives can be made relevant in other ways than by one's environment, though it does so in such a way as to keep the demands on our discriminative powers realistic. That becoming aware of an alternative can make that alternative relevant explains why raising an alternative in a conversational context can make evidential demands on one. Suppose I claim to know that the creature over there is a goldfinch, and you respond by introducing the suggestion that it might be a hologram goldfinch (to keep the example as clean as possible, let us stipulate that you don't offer any grounds for thinking that this alternative might obtain; you just simply mention it as an alternative). I may well tell you to get lost, and we may well grant that I would be right to do so (you've certainly offended against some normal constraints on good conversation). Still, if I hadn't considered the possibility before, I should now, since I now know that this is an alternative to what I take myself to know. Moreover, in considering the alternative, I should be able to rule it out. If ruling it out meant having the relevant perceptual discriminative capacity, then knowledge would be in short supply with people like you around, but if it merely means having appropriate favouring evidence, then meeting this requirement should be fairly straightforward. For I have all kinds of good reasons for thinking that what I am looking at is a goldfinch rather than a hologram goldfinch.[19]

This simple distinction regarding how alternatives can become relevant—and the distinction between favouring and discriminating epistemic support that underlies it—can, I think, remove much of the impetus for one key thread of revisionistic thought in epistemology during the last thirty or so years since Dretske published his seminal article on why we should reject the closure principle. One aspect of this thread of revisionistic thought is the Dretskean thesis that the principle of closure must be rejected, but it is not the only aspect. Now is not the place to explore this claim fully, but let me at least offer a 'taster' of what I have in mind.

Consider again the contrastivist account of knowledge described earlier. As we saw above, according to this proposal knowledge is to be understood as essentially involving discrimination, such that knowing a proposition boils down to having the relevant discriminatory capacities. The distinction between favouring and discriminating epistemic support clearly removes a central plank of support for this view. After all, one principal motivation for the position comes from the intuition that it is problematic to suppose that Zula is able to know that what she is looking at is not a cleverly disguised mule (and thereby know that what she is looking at is a zebra rather than a cleverly disguised mule). But as we have demonstrated here, this supposition is only problematic provided one already understands such knowledge in terms of Zula's possession of the relevant discriminatory powers. It is thus highly contentious to move from this 'intuition' to the claim that knowledge should be understood contrastively, and thereby essentially in terms of discriminatory powers.

It should be clear even from this brief discussion of contrastivism that the proposal sketched here has ramifications for any revisionist account of knowledge which takes as part of the philosophical 'data' that needs to be explained the fact that agents like Zula in zebra-style cases lack knowledge of the entailed proposition (at least once the relevant error-possibility is raised), for it is precisely this 'intuition' which is shown to be unmotivated by this proposal.[20] Recognizing the distinction between favouring and discriminating epistemic support thus has important implications not just for our understanding of the relevant alternatives intuition and the relationship between perceptual knowledge and discrimination, but also for contemporary epistemology more generally.

§7. Favouring versus Discriminating Epistemic Support and Epistemological Disjunctivism

So far in part two, epistemological disjunctivism has mostly been in the background. As noted at several junctures above, there is a good reason for this, since the main thesis that is being propounded here regarding favouring and discriminating epistemic support is not meant to be hostage to the truth of any particular epistemological proposal, much less a controversial proposal like epistemological disjunctivism. Nonetheless, as we will now see, recognizing this distinction between favouring and discriminating epistemic support is crucial to motivating the epistemological disjunctivist position.

Recall the distinguishability problem described in part one. This concerned the fact that if one does have reflective access to factive reasons in the good+ case, then it is hard to see how one can reconcile this claim with the undeniable truth there are parallel introspectively indistinguishable bad cases (of any of the four types distinguished in §5 of part one) in which one lacks a factive reason but where, nonetheless, one continues to blamelessly suppose that one possesses it. For if, in the good+ case, one has reflective access to the relevant factive reason, then why doesn't it follow that one can introspectively distinguish between the good+ case and the corresponding bad case after all, contrary to intuition? For in the good+ case there *is* something reflectively accessible to one which is not reflectively accessible in the corresponding bad case—*viz.*, the target factive reason. Accordingly, it seems it should by epistemological disjunctivist lights be very easy to introspectively distinguish between good+ and bad cases, since all one needs to do is see if the relevant reason is reflectively available. In short, the distinguishability problem is that it is difficult to understand how epistemological disjunctivism can account for the apparently undeniable fact that there are pairs of deceived and non-deceived cases of the sort just described which are introspectively indistinguishable.

We can express the distinguishability problem more formally as follows:

The Distinguishability Problem

(DP1) In the good+ case, S perceptually knows that p in virtue of possessing reflectively accessible factive rational support for her belief that p. [Premise]

(DP2) S can know by reflection alone that it is only in the good+ case that she possesses reflectively accessible factive rational support for her belief that p. [Premise]

(DPC1) In the good+ case, S is in a position to competently deduce, and thereby know, that she is in the good+ case (and thus not in a corresponding bad case). [From (DP1), (DP2)]

(DPC2) In the good+ case, S can introspectively distinguish between the good+ case and a corresponding bad case. [From (DPC1)]

The premises of this argument—i.e., (DP1) and (DP2)—constitute unavoidable commitments on the part of the epistemological disjunctivist, and yet with these premises in play the intermediate conclusion of the argument— i.e., (DPC1)—seems to straightforwardly follow. The problem, however, is that this intermediate conclusion seems to entail the ultimate conclusion that our subject is able to introspectively distinguish between the good+ case and corresponding bad cases (i.e., (DPC2)). After all, if one can indeed come to know through competent deduction that one is in the good+ case as opposed to a corresponding bad case (as (DPC1) maintains), then how is that different from being able to introspectively distinguish between a good+ and a corresponding bad case (as (DPC2) maintains)? And yet epistemological disjunctivists are clearly also unavoidably committed to denying that agents can introspectively distinguish between good+ and corresponding bad cases. The distinguishability problem is thus in effect a *reductio* of the epistemological disjunctivist position.

The distinction between favouring and discriminating epistemic support offers us a way out of this problem. Before we get to this point, however, a comment on (DPC1) is in order, since as it stands this (intermediate) conclusion might be thought to represent a variant of the access problem for epistemological disjunctivism that we examined in part one (§7), whereby this view seems to allow us to gain non-empirical knowledge of specific empirical propositions. Something very similar seems to be happening here, in that the agent appears to have an entirely reflective route to knowledge of a specific empirical proposition (in this case, that she is in the good+ case).

As we saw in part one, the access problem can be avoided once we recognize how the putative exclusively reflective knowledge in question is essentially based on empirical rational support (and hence is not exclusively reflective knowledge at all). The same diagnosis applies here, though the case is a little more complex. The key thing to notice is that (DP1) is only true if S's belief that p is based on the *empirical* epistemic support provided by her seeing that p. This is crucial, since it means that a central plank in the inference to (DPC1) involves empirical epistemic support. Clearly, then, S's putative knowledge in (DPC1) that she is in the good+ case cannot be exclusively reflective, since it rests in part on this empirical epistemic support.

We noted in our discussion of the access problem in part one that all that the proponent of this difficulty will be able to motivate is this claim:

(APC″) In the good+ case, S can know by reflection alone that her reason for believing the specific empirical proposition p is the factive empirical reason R which entails p.

And we argued that this claim is benign, since it merely highlights that if you allow, with epistemological disjunctivism, that subjects can have reflective access to their factive empirical reasons (in the good+ case anyway), then subjects who in addition know (by reflection) what it means for an empirical reason to be factive are also thereby in a position to know by reflection alone that they are in possession of a factive empirical reason which entails the target proposition.

A similar point applies here, although we have to adapt the claim in order to accommodate the fact that in the current version of the access problem the agent is not making an inference to the specific empirical proposition at issue in the first premise (i.e., p), but to a distinct (albeit still empirical) proposition—*viz.*, that she is in the good+ case. Even so, the adapted version of this claim is still benign:

(*) In the good+ case, S can know by reflection alone that her reason for believing the specific empirical proposition p is the factive empirical reason R which entails that she is in the good+ case.

Again, this claim is innocuous because it merely highlights that if you allow, with epistemological disjunctivism, that subjects can have reflective access to their factive empirical reasons (in the good+ case anyway), then subjects who in addition know (by reflection) that such reasons are only reflectively available in the good+ case are also thereby in a position to know by reflection alone that they are in possession of a factive empirical reason which entails that they are in the good case. But this is a very different claim to that which is at issue in the access problem, since it does not imply that one can gain exclusive reflective knowledge of the target empirical proposition (in this instance that one is in the good+ case).

With this point in mind, let us return to considering how the distinction between favouring and discriminating epistemic support can enable us to avoid the distinguishability problem. Consider again the Zula case, but this time let us feed epistemological disjunctivism into the story as well. To begin with, then, we have Zula in a good+ case which is both subjectively and objectively epistemically good. According to epistemological disjunctivism her veridical perception in these circumstances ensures that she sees that there is a zebra before her (p), and this forms the reflectively accessible rational basis for her perceptual knowledge of this proposition. *Ex hypothesi*, however, she cannot tell the difference between this scenario and a parallel introspectively indistinguishable bad scenario. For simplicity, let us specifically consider a bad++ scenario where Zula's perception is no longer veridical and where the circumstances are objectively epistemically bad such that she does not see that p. That she is presently looking at a cleverly disguised mule would be an example of a bad++ scenario.

As things stand, we have no reason for supposing that Zula forms any view about the specific bad++ scenario that we have just described. In particular, there is no reason why she would have formed the belief that the creature before her is not a cleverly disguised mule. The interesting question for us, however, is how it would affect Zula's epistemic situation were she to consider this specific error-possibility. There are two ways in which this can come about. In the first it is by Zula simply considering this error-possibility *qua* error-possibility—i.e., without any good epistemic basis for thinking that this error-possibility should be taken into account. In the second it is by Zula acquiring an epistemic basis for taking this error-possibility seriously. For now, let us imagine that the situation fits the former rather than the latter description (we will consider what happens when the situation fits the latter description in a moment).

With the situation so described—and bearing in mind that Zula is in the good+ case, and hence has a reflectively accessible factive rational basis for her belief—there ought to be no problem with supposing that she is in a position to competently deduce that she is in the good+ case (and thus that she is not in the bad++ case), at least provided she is aware of the relevant entailment. The conclusion of the argument above therefore goes through, and goes through even despite it being the case that this conclusion seems to conflict with the apparently undeniable fact that Zula cannot introspectively distinguish between the good+ case that she is in and the corresponding bad++ case.

Let's look again at the crucial (putative) entailment from the intermediate conclusion of the argument at issue in the distinguishability problem to the ultimate conclusion:

(DPC1) In the good+ case, S is in a position to competently deduce, and thereby know, that she is in the good+ case (and thus not in a corresponding bad case). [From (DP1), (DP2)]

(DPC2) In the good+ case, S can introspectively distinguish between the good+ case and a corresponding bad case. [From (DPC1)]

The first thing to note is that as it stands (DPC2) is not quite right. For as we have just seen in the Zula example we have used to illustrate the distinguishability problem, Zula doesn't come to know that she is in the good+ case rather than the corresponding bad++ case merely via introspection. Instead, she must also undertake additional a priori reasoning. Strictly speaking, then, what follows from (DPC1) is thus not (DPC2) but rather the slightly weaker (DPC2′), where 'reflectively distinguish' means 'distinguish solely via either introspection and/or a priori reasoning':

(DPC2′) In the good+ case, S can reflectively distinguish between the good+ case and a corresponding bad case. [From (DPC1)]

Now this might be thought to be merely splitting hairs since, aside from anything else, isn't (DPC2′) just as contentious as (DPC2)? That is, isn't the thought that there is *any* non-empirical route by which an agent can come to distinguish between good+ cases and corresponding bad cases in tension with the claim that such cases are by their nature indistinguishable? We will return to this issue.

Even with the conclusion of the distinguishability argument reformulated along the lines of (DPC2'), it is still problematic. For notice that given
the general distinction between favouring and discriminating epistemic
support that we have motivated above we should be alert to an important
ambiguity in how this claim can be understood. In short, given this
distinction the very idea of two scenarios being introspectively (/reflec-
tively) indistinguishable is ambiguous between a reading in terms of
discriminating epistemic support and a reading in terms of favouring
epistemic support.

In order to see this, consider again our discussion of the Zula case from
earlier. We noted there that there is an important difference between a
case in which the epistemic support for Zula's conviction that what she
sees is a zebra rather than a cleverly disguised mule is discriminating rather
than merely favouring. In the former case, Zula can perceptually discriminate between the two scenarios in question (i.e., she can perceptually
discriminate between the objects at issue in those scenarios), perhaps
because she has made special checks, or has special expertise. In the latter
case, Zula cannot perceptually discriminate between these two scenarios,
but she can nonetheless know that the one scenario obtains but not the
other in virtue of the evidence that she has available to her which favours
this scenario over the alternative. More generally, the moral of our
discussion above was that there is a sense in which one can know the
difference which doesn't imply that one knows the difference through the
exercise of a discriminative capacity.

Here is the crux. The ultimate conclusion of the distinguishability
problem—i.e., (DPC2')—merely demands that the subject can reflectively
distinguish between the good+ case and a corresponding bad case. But
one can satisfy *that* demand merely by being in possession of favouring
epistemic support with regard to the pair of cases in question, and by
making the relevant competent deductions. One will thereby be able to
know, via introspection and a priori reasoning alone, that one is in the
good+ case rather than the corresponding bad case even though one
cannot perceptually discriminate between these two scenarios (i.e., even
though one cannot perceptually discriminate between the objects at issue
in those two scenarios).

More specifically, the idea is that Zula, if she is indeed in possession of
factive reflectively accessible rational support in favour of her knowledge
that *p*, has grounds available to her which, when supplemented with the

relevant competent deductions anyway, ensure that she can know that she is in the good+ case rather than the corresponding bad++ case. This entails that the ultimate conclusion of the distinguishability problem— which we have reformulated as (DPC2′)—is true. But it doesn't at all follow from this that Zula thereby has a discriminate capacity which enables her to perceptually discriminate between the target good+ and bad++ cases (i.e., between the objects at issue in those cases). After all, the way in which Zula is coming to know that she is in the good+ case rather than the corresponding bad++ case does not advert to a perceptual discriminative capacity to tell the target good+ and bad++ cases apart at all (i.e., to tell apart zebras from cleverly disguised mules), but is purely to do with her ability to draw competent deductions from her relevant factive reasons. In short, the epistemic support she possesses for her knowledge that she is in the good+ case rather than the corresponding bad++ case is specifically favouring rather than discriminating epistemic support.

It follows that (DPC2′) is not nearly as problematic for epistemological disjunctivism as it first appears, so long as it is understood correctly. That is, we can accommodate the idea that Zula is unable to perceptually discriminate between the two target scenarios (i.e., because she cannot distinguish between the objects at issue in those scenarios), while nonetheless granting—in line with (DPC2′)—that there is a way in which she can nonetheless reflectively distinguish between them.

Moreover, the importance of the distinction made above between introspective distinguishability and reflective distinguishability should now be very clear. For in the context of epistemological disjunctivism, which allows that agents in good+ cases can have reflectively accessible factive rational support for their beliefs, it clearly is vital to draw a distinction between cases which are merely reflectively distinguishable as opposed to being introspectively distinguishable. This is because the very nature of such reflectively accessible factive rational support means that there is a non-empirical route, via competent deductions, through which one can come to distinguish between scenarios which are introspectively indistinguishable.

Take the Zula case, for example. We have seen that there is a reflective (and thus non-empirical) route through which Zula, by undertaking competent deductions which make use of the factive rational support available to her, can come to distinguish between the good+ case that she is in and the corresponding bad++ case. Note, however, that it remains true even by epistemological disjunctivist lights that even in the good+ case Zula cannot distinguish via introspection alone between the good+ case and the corresponding bad++ case. Instead, further a priori reasoning is in addition required. Thus, the fact that Zula can reflectively distinguish between these two scenarios is not in tension with the fact that she is unable to introspectively distinguish between them.

Before we move on, a further comment about Zula's knowledge in this case is required. In our discussion of the Zula example in §6 above where we explored the two-tiered relevant alternatives theory it was stipulated that Zula needed to adduce independent grounds in order to come know that she was not the victim of the relevant error-possibility, even though, as just now, we were supposing that the error-possibility was merely introduced to Zula and not at all epistemically supported (or, at least, we were supposing that it need not have an epistemic basis). If that's right, however, then one might wonder why Zula doesn't have to adduce an independent epistemic basis for her belief by the epistemological disjunctivist's lights as well.

Notice, though, that if we are able to help ourselves to the idea that Zula has not only reflectively accessible rational support for her belief that p, but moreover reflectively accessible rational support for her belief that p which *entails* p, then this changes the dialectical situation entirely. In the version of the Zula case that we looked at in §6 Zula had no reflectively accessible rational support which spoke to the error-possibility in question, and hence it was important that even if the error-possibility was merely considered she should nonetheless be able to adduce adequate independent grounds before dismissing this error-possibility. If one is in possession of reflectively accessible *factive* rational support, however, then clearly one's grounds *do* speak to the error-possibility in question, since they entail its falsity.[21] If one has no epistemic basis for taking the error-possibility seriously, then the mere fact that one is in possession of such factive rational support ought to suffice to enable one to rationally exclude such a possibility and thereby know that it does not obtain.

The situation is complicated somewhat if we consider an example of the Zula case where the agent is given good grounds for supposing that the error-possibility in question should be taken seriously—where, for example, she is given good grounds for supposing that the creature before her is a cleverly disguised mule (and hence grounds for thinking that she is in a bad++ case). Here it *does* seem plausible to suppose that Zula should have an independent basis for dismissing this error-possibility, and shouldn't simply appeal to her reflectively accessible factive reason. This is because in this case Zula is in effect being given grounds for supposing that she *doesn't* see that *p*, and hence unless she can in turn rationally respond to this ground for doubt—thereby neutralizing its negative epistemic force— then it seems that she can no longer simply take herself to be seeing that *p*.

Going back to the taxonomy of good and bad cases that we offered in part one, it should be clear that what is happening here is that we are in effect moving from a good+ case to a merely good case, since Zula is now in possession of an undefeated defeater for her belief that *p*. As we noted in part one, although it remains true in such cases that the agent is in circumstances which are objectively epistemically good and her perception is reliable, there is now a subjective epistemic 'badness' in play such that as matters stand the agent is not in a position to responsibly believe that *p* but should instead defer judgement until the defeater has been defeated. Once we realize that the agent is now in the merely good case, however, then this has an immediate effect on the distinguishability problem, since it now follows that the first premise of that problem, which explicitly states that the agent is in the good+ case, is false.[22]

Moreover, remember that it is not an incidental feature of this way of formulating the distinguishability problem that the agent is in the good+ case. As argued in part one, although it remains true in a merely good case that the agent sees that *p*, it is no part of the epistemological disjunctivist thesis to claim that this is reflectively accessible to the agent. Accordingly, one cannot run the distinguishability problem without stipulating that the agent is in the good+ case, since it is only if she is in this case that she has reflective access to the factive reason which is needed to get the problem underway.

In any case, for the kind of bad++ cases that we are envisaging (and unlike radical sceptical error-possibilities, which we will be looking at in part three), the neutralizing grounds required to defeat the defeater in play should be easy for the agent to acquire, and hence it ought to be unproblematic for Zula to transform this good case back into a good+ case. If Zula is even modestly rationally sophisticated, then there will, after all, be a wealth of background information available to her which could rationally support her dismissal of the cleverly disguised mule hypothesis. She would then be entitled to continue supposing that the rational basis for her knowledge that p is that she sees that p.[23] The presence of such a defeater thus should not be a rational bar to her competently deducing thereby that she is not in the bad++ case. Hence, in this case (DPC2′) goes through, though as we noted above this is not problematic once we understand this claim correctly.

The distinction between favouring and discriminating epistemic support—a distinction which we saw is motivated entirely independently of epistemological disjunctivism—thus provides a way of blocking the distinguishability problem for epistemological disjunctivism. Given that this is the last of the three outstanding *prima facie* problems of epistemological disjunctivism raised in part one, this demonstrates that the position is eminently viable, and hence should not be dismissed out of hand on account of the serious difficulties that it faces.

We noted earlier in our discussion of this distinction that the problem of radical scepticism creates a great deal of 'noise' when it comes to contemporary thinking about these issues. This is especially so when it comes to the epistemological disjunctivist's use of this distinction, as we will see below. For while the epistemological disjunctivist can make appeal to this distinction in order to accommodate the relevant conclusions of the distinguishability problem while avoiding paradox, bringing in the topic of radical scepticism adds a new layer to this problem. We thus need to consider the problem of radical scepticism and its bearing on epistemological disjunctivism in its own right, and this will be the concern of part three.

As we will see in the next part, however, it is possible for epistemological disjunctivism to trade on its distinctive features to offer a uniquely direct response to the problem of radical scepticism, one that has all the merits of an epistemic internalist treatment of this difficulty but which lacks the usual drawbacks of approaches of this sort. Given the other attractions of the view that we have expounded, and given also that we have seen that this position is not subject to the kinds of obvious challenges that can reasonably be laid against it, it follows that epistemological disjunctivism is a proposal that we should take very seriously indeed.

Notes to Part Two

1. Of course, not all perceptual knowledge is knowledge of objects. For example, some perceptual knowledge is of distances. I take it, however, that perceptual knowledge is paradigmatically about objects, and so in order to simplify matters in what follows I will set these other types of perceptual knowledge to one side. (If one prefers, then one can think of the type of perceptual knowledge at issue as specifically *objectual* perceptual knowledge.) Moreover, in order to keep matters as simple as possible, in what follows we will be focusing on cases of perceptual knowledge where there is a single object at issue.

2. Notice that I am understanding the ordering of possible worlds in the standard way in terms of their similarity to the actual world. See especially Stalnaker (1968) and Lewis (1973). A different way of understanding relevance is in probabilistic terms, such that what makes an alternative irrelevant is the fact that it concerns low-probability possibilities (e.g., hologram goldfinches). Although the difference between the two views is not particularly important here (because, for the most part, low probability possibilities are far-off possibilities, and high-probability possibilities are close possibilities), I favour the first sort of proposal because of the fact that low-probability events can occur in nearby possible worlds (think, for example, of lottery wins). In such cases, I maintain that the modal nearness of the possibility will make it relevant even despite the fact that it is a low-probability event. For a defence of a version of the probabilistic account, see Cohen (1988).

3. Note that one would need to supplement this principle in various ways if one wished to provide a complete account of perceptual knowledge (even granting the caveats noted in endnote 1 above). For example, the class of relevant alternatives will need to be extended beyond the not-ϕ alternatives, since there will clearly be some alternatives which are incompatible with knowing that ϕ even while being compatible with ϕ (think, for example, of error-possibilities involving dreaming). Even so, I think it is reasonable to refer to such a proposal as an 'account' of perceptual knowledge, even though it is incomplete in these ways, since the claim is that perceptual knowledge *essentially* consists in the satisfaction of this condition (i.e., setting some peripheral considerations to one side, if one satisfies this condition, then one possesses perceptual knowledge).

4. Notice as well that this account of perceptual knowledge is very anti-intellectualist, which might also be thought to be an advantage of the proposal. For example, a small child may lack the concept of a horse and yet, because she can nevertheless perceptually discriminate between zebras and horses, she can still come to know that what she is looking at is a zebra.

5. This is a different—and, I think, more plausible—way of understanding the closure principle to how Dretske (1970; cf. Dretske 2005a) understands it, though nothing hangs on this difference here. This formulation of the closure principle is essentially that offered by Williamson (2000a, 117) and Hawthorne (2005, 29). For the most recent critical discussion of the closure principle, see the exchange between Dretske (2005a; 2005b) and Hawthorne (2005).

6. I take it as obvious that this problem isn't peculiar to the zebra case (or the goldfinch case for that matter), since the problem straightforwardly generalizes to lots of other cases. Consider Barney, who is presently looking (in normal circumstances) at a barn and, on this basis, comes to know that what he is looking at is a barn. Suppose, however, that Barney knows that if what he is looking at is a barn, then it isn't a barn façade, and competently deduces on this basis that he is not looking at a barn façade. He thereby knows, given the closure principle, that what he is looking at is a barn rather than a barn façade. We can stipulate, however, that Barney has no special evidence or expertise in this regard. He has not checked to see whether this is a barn façade, nor is he skilled enough to be able to tell, just by looking straight on, whether the structure before him is a barn rather than a barn façade. In short, he cannot perceptually discriminate between barns and barn façades. So how then can it be that he knows that what he is looking at is a barn rather than a barn façade, which is what the closure principle seems to demand?

7. This is not the place to explore these points further. For a defence of the first claim—that the sensitivity principle, properly understood, does not generate the kinds of closure-failure that it is meant to—see Williams (1991, ch. 9) and Black (2002). For a defence of the second claim—that a sensitivity-based epistemology is in any case in conflict with the core relevant alternatives intuition—see Pritchard (2002a; 2005b, chs. 2–3). There are lots of other objections that have been levelled against sensitivity-based views, of course. For a recent statement of one such objection, see Sosa (1999).

8. For another prominent defence of contrastivism, see Sinnott-Armstrong (2006).

9. For a contrastivist defence of closure-type inferences, see Schaffer (2006). For a critique, see Kelp (2011). I discuss the contrastivist account in more detail in Pritchard (2008a).

10. Recall that we are specifically focusing on simple cases of perceptual knowledge which concern a single object. See endnote 1.

11. As Dretske exegesis, this is not quite right, since Dretske (1970, 1016) not only appeals to Zula's lack of the relevant discriminative abilities in his argument against the closure principle, but also maintains that she lacks the required supporting evidence for knowledge of the entailed proposition. Crucially, though, the kind of supporting evidence that Dretske thinks would be

required is evidence for thinking that she can make the relevant discriminations, such as the evidence she would gain by making special checks, and so
this second aspect to his critique of the closure principle is ultimately just a
variation on the first. I consider the import that such 'discriminating' evidence
has for this issue below.

12. The idea that knowledge is essentially non-lucky true belief is one of the
recurring motifs of epistemology. The main stimulus for the contemporary
discussion of an anti-luck epistemology of this sort is Unger (1968). For a
recent defence of anti-luck epistemology—one which ties such an epistemology to the kind of safety-based accounts of knowledge advocated by Sosa
(1999; 2000) and others—see Pritchard (2005b; 2007a; cf. Pritchard 2012a;
2013).

13. While this formulation of the transmission principle is my own, it shares
essential features with the principle as it is usually formulated in the contemporary literature. For a classic exchange on the transmission principle, see
Davies (2004) and Wright (2004a). One complication that I will be setting
aside in what follows is that one might plausibly maintain that simply undertaking the relevant deduction enhances one's evidence set. Klein (1995), for
example, holds a view of roughly this sort. If that's right, however, then it
could be that it is only one's *enhanced* evidence set which is sufficient for
knowledge of the deduced proposition in some cases. Since the evidential
worry highlighted by evidential transmission that we are discussing here
concerns the fact that the agent's evidence for believing the deduced proposition is *nowhere near* sufficient for knowledge of that proposition, I think we can
safely ignore this potential complication.

14. A version of this principle is also known in the literature as the 'underdetermination' principle. For a more detailed discussion of this principle, including
its logical relationship to the closure principle, see Pritchard (2005a, ch. 4;
2005c). See also Yalçin (1992); Brueckner (1994); Cohen (1998); and Vogel
(2004).

15. Stine (1976) defends the closure principle by in effect restricting the application of the two evidential principles just mentioned. This is because she
accommodates the oddity of allowing that an agent can know the denials of
irrelevant alternatives like the cleverly disguised mule alternative by claiming,
contrary to intuition, that such knowledge is non-evidential. That is, while she
agrees with Dretske that Zula has no evidence for believing the cleverly
disguised mule hypothesis to be false, she nevertheless argues that because
this is an irrelevant alternative this does not prevent her from knowing this to
be the case, since one can know that irrelevant alternatives are false without
evidence. The way she retains the closure principle thus compels her to
restrict, in a counterintuitive way, the application of the evidential and

favouring principles. As I argue below, however, such a concession can be avoided if one understands Zula's evidential position in the right way.

16. I take it that the same applies to those alternatives which one is not aware of but which one should be aware of (e.g., where one's lack of awareness is due to one's close-mindedness, say). In order to bracket this complication, in what follows we will assume, where relevant, that agents are always aware of the error-possibilities that they should be aware of.

17. It is important to note that this proposal is very different to a superficially similar view defended by Cohen (1988). While Cohen also makes the point that an agent like Zula might be in possession of background evidence that would enable her to rationally dismiss the cleverly disguised mule hypothesis, he makes the crucial error of supposing that being in possession of this evidence is required for *anyone* to come to know that what they are looking at is a zebra. But this is a far too restrictive account of knowledge, and certainly does not conform to the original aspirations of a relevant alternatives account of perceptual knowledge, a view that is meant to set the bar for perceptual knowledge potentially quite low. Imagine, for example, a small child looking at a zebra in a zoo in normal conditions (there's no deception going on, no reason to think that there is deception going on, no far-fetched error-possibilities have been raised, and so on). This child can perfectly well perceptually discriminate zebras from other things that might plausibly be around (horses, litter bins, etc.). But we would not expect such a child to have the kind of collateral evidence available to her that Cohen wants to make a prerequisite of perceptual knowledge. Surely, though, the child knows that what she sees is a zebra? In any case, one of the advantages of my approach is that it is perfectly consistent with allowing knowledge in cases like this. Moreover, there is no need on my view to postulate the kind of attributer contextualism about 'knows' that Cohen endorses in the light of the zebra case. For him, what happens when we consider the cleverly disguised mule hypothesis is that we enter a high-standards context in which the assertion 'Zula knows that what she is looking at is a zebra' is no longer true. On my view, in contrast, we can explain what is going on without any appeal to the context-sensitivity of 'knows'. Instead, all that is being appealed to is the fact that becoming aware of an error-possibility can raise the evidential burden required in order to know, albeit in such a way that this burden is usually very easily met. But this fact no more indicates that 'knows' is a context-sensitive term than the fact that becoming aware of a defeater to something that one believes raises the evidential burden for knowledge. For further discussion of the differences between my proposal and that put forward by Cohen, see Pritchard (2010).

18. In Dretske's original discussion of this example, for instance, he directly moves to the issue of whether Zula can legitimately claim to know that what she is

looking at is not a cleverly disguised mule. That it would be inappropriate for Zula to (flatly) make a claim of this sort does not indicate that such a claim would be false, however, especially given the point just mentioned that flat-out claims to know typically imply that the asserter has relevant discriminatory epistemic support in favour of what she asserts. I discuss the relationship between appropriate claims to know and discriminatory epistemic support in more detail in Pritchard (2007b; 2008b).

19. One potential objection to the view defended here is that it makes knowledge 'unstable', in the sense that it can be easily lost. That the relevant favouring evidence is usually easily available, however, explains why this is not in fact the case. For while it is true that this view allows that a subject can have perceptual knowledge even while lacking the relevant favouring evidence, and hence concedes that such an agent's knowledge will be unstable in the sense that it could be lost once the error-possibility in question in raised, such cases are bound to be relatively rare. After all, it is central to the view defended here that it takes very little by way of intellectual sophistication to be able to possess the relevant favouring evidence and bring it to bear on the error-possibility in hand, and so we can reasonably expect that in a wide range of cases one's knowledge will exhibit no such 'instability'. Moreover, that knowledge should be unstable in these special cases is surely far from counterintuitive. Note too that the view of knowledge in play here is entirely compatible with the idea that all knowledge (even the 'unstable' knowledge just described) is stable in the sense of being *safe*—i.e., it involves a belief in the target proposition that could not have easily been false.

20. For example, such an assumption is clearly motivating, in part at least, some of the main attributer contextualist proposals with regard to knowledge ascriptions. For an explicit instance of this, see Cohen (1988; 2000). See also DeRose (1995) and Lewis (1996). I think it is also arguable that the related subject-sensitive (/interest-relative) invariantist views that have recently been defended in the literature—see especially Hawthorne (2004) and Stanley (2005)—are in part motivated by this assumption too, though this is a much harder case to make. (One can find the beginnings of such a case in Pritchard (2007c).)

21. Interestingly, notice that this can be true even if one is dealing with an error-possibility that is compatible with the truth of the target proposition, as might happen, for example, if one were in a merely bad+ case (recall that in such situations the perception is veridical). For in bad+ cases it still remains true that one lacks the relevant reflectively accessible factive reason, and hence the possession of such a reason entails that one is not in such a predicament. In order to keep the discussion as straightforward as possible, I will set aside this complication here.

22. I am assuming here that the defeater in question is a misleading defeater, but of course it could be that the grounds for doubt in question are not misleading at all. Note, however, that if this is the situation then it follows that the agent is in an even weaker epistemic position than the (merely) good case. The point I am making thus still goes through.

23. It is an interesting question whether in such a case Zula's seeing that p suffices for her to know that p, or whether the additional rational support offered by the defeater–defeater also plays a supporting role. I take no stand on this issue here. For a classic discussion of this issue, see Plantinga (1986).

PART THREE

Radical Scepticism

Introductory Remarks

We saw in part two that there is a general epistemological distinction between favouring and discriminating epistemic support which the epistemological disjunctivist can appeal to in order to evade the distinguishability problem. We also noted, however, that while this distinction can help one to evade the problem posed by 'Zula-style' cases, it doesn't have a straightforward application to the problem of radical scepticism. This point will be further illustrated below when we will see how the epistemological disjunctivist cannot evade the problem of radical scepticism merely by appeal to this distinction. More work is thus required if we want to fashion a plausible anti-sceptical response out of epistemological disjunctivism. The good news, however, is that this can be done, and the task of this part is to outline how.

In order to focus our attention in this regard, we will be looking at the kind of crude 'Moorean' anti-sceptical strategy that the epistemological disjunctivist anti-sceptical line appears to most closely resemble. As we will see, the anti-sceptical position made available by an epistemological disjunctivist epistemology is in fact far subtler than it first appears.

§1. Radical Scepticism

The standard way of motivating radical scepticism in the contemporary epistemological literature is via a simple two-step argument. The first step involves making appeal to radical sceptical hypotheses that depict scenarios in which we are undetectably subject to massive cognitive error. Since we've already introduced the 'brain-in-a-vat' (BIV) radical sceptical scenario in part two (see §5), we'll use this hypothesis here. The claim made on this score is that it follows from the very nature of radical sceptical hypotheses like the BIV hypothesis that one cannot possibly know that they are false. For how would one go about coming to know that they didn't obtain? For example, given that the life inside the vat is meant to be indistinguishable from ordinary (non-envatted) life, how would one exclude this possibility?

That we are unable to know the denials of radical sceptical hypotheses does not by itself motivate radical scepticism, however, since on the face of it our failure to know this specific class of propositions is entirely consistent with our having widespread knowledge. Take, for example, my putative knowledge that I have two hands. Why can't it be both true that I know this 'everyday' proposition and that I lack knowledge of the 'anti-sceptical' proposition that I am not a BIV?

What we need to motivate radical scepticism is thus some further claim which ensures that our failure to know the denials of radical sceptical hypotheses undermines our knowledge of everyday propositions too. This is where the closure principle that we saw in part two (§2) comes into play:

The Closure Principle
If S knows that ϕ, and S competently deduces ψ from ϕ (thereby coming to believe that ψ while retaining her knowledge that ϕ), then S knows that ψ.

As we saw there, it is hard to see how this principle could fail. The problem, however, is that with this principle in play one can pretty straightforwardly draw the necessary connection between an inability to know the denials of radical sceptical hypothesis and a lack of everyday knowledge. After all, having hands is manifestly inconsistent with being a (handless) BIV, and hence if one did know that one has two hands then one ought to be able to reason, in line with the closure principle, to knowledge that that one is not a BIV. That is, for the rationally articulate anyway, knowledge that one has hands entails knowledge that one is not a BIV.[1] But the radical sceptic has (they claim) just demonstrated to us that it is *impossible* to know that one is not a BIV. It thus follows that the antecedent of this conditional must be false, such that one cannot know that one has two hands. And what applies to one's knowledge that one has two hands can of course be extended to any number of other everyday propositions too (one would just need to alter the radical sceptical hypothesis in play accordingly). Radical scepticism ensues.

We are now in a position to formulate our radical sceptical argument:

Radical Scepticism
(S1) I am unable to know the denials of radical sceptical hypotheses.

(S2) If I am unable to know the denials of radical sceptical hypotheses, then I am unable to possess much of the everyday knowledge which I typically attribute to myself.

(SC) I am unable to possess much of the everyday knowledge which I typically attribute to myself.

The motivation for (S1) is meant to come from reflecting on the nature of radical sceptical hypotheses. The motivation for (S2) is meant to come from the highly plausible closure principle. And since (S1) and (S2) entail (SC), we have thus motivated radical scepticism.

In order to simplify our discussion we will focus on a more concrete rendering of the radical sceptical argument, one which is specifically formulated in terms of a particular radical sceptical hypothesis and a particular item of putative everyday knowledge which is called into question by the argument:

BIV-Based Radical Scepticism
(BIV1) I don't know that I'm not a BIV.
(BIV2) If I know that I have two hands, then I know that I'm not a BIV.
(BIVC) I don't know that I have two hands.

As before, the motivation for (BIV1) is meant to come from reflecting on the nature of radical sceptical hypotheses and the motivation for (BIV2) is meant to come from the highly plausible closure principle.

There are some further differences between this BIV-based formulation of radical scepticism and the more general formulation that are worthy of note. First, notice that for ease of expression this is a 'demodalized' rendering of the radical sceptical argument. The claim made here is not that we are *unable* to know that we are not BIVs, and thus that we are *unable* to know the target everyday proposition, but just that such knowledge is, in both cases, lacking. The demodalized radical sceptical conclusion should be strong enough for our purposes. Right now the epistemic conditions for knowing that I have two hands are about as good as they ever could be for knowing such a contingent empirical proposition, so if the radical sceptic is right that such knowledge is lacking then I ought be very concerned by radical scepticism indeed.

Second, notice that the second premise of the BIV-based argument is formulated in a different way to the second premise of the more general radical sceptical argument. Rather than focus on how a lack of knowledge of the denials of radical sceptical hypotheses leads to a lack of knowledge of everyday propositions, as in (S2), (BIV2) focuses instead on how knowledge of everyday propositions leads to knowledge of the denials of radical sceptical hypotheses. The difference is purely presentational, and nothing substantive hangs on it. As we will see in a moment, formulating the second premise in this way is simply more useful when it comes to evaluating the merits of a certain kind of anti-sceptical proposal.

Finally, third, notice that the conclusion of this argument falls short of a full-blown radical sceptical thesis. It is, after all, a further step to conclude from one's lack of knowledge that one has two hands that the everyday knowledge which one typically ascribes to oneself is also lacking. But (BIVC), while weaker than (SC), should be strong enough for our purposes. As just noted, the epistemic conditions right now for knowing that I have two hands are about as good as they ever could be for knowing any contingent empirical proposition. Accordingly, if we do not know a proposition like this then it is natural to conclude that we there is not very much that we can know. As a consequence, if (BIVC) is true then we should be very alarmed indeed.[2]

§2. Mooreanism

Consider now the following three-part response to radical scepticism, a response which mirrors in key respects the 'commonsense' proposal often ascribed to G. E. Moore (and which is regarded with almost wholesale derision). Call this anti-sceptical proposal, *Mooreanism*.[3] The first part of this anti-sceptical response is to focus on an everyday proposition which we paradigmatically take ourselves to know, such as that one has two hands, and to insist that we do indeed know this proposition. The second part of the response is to note that since this everyday proposition is manifestly inconsistent with the target radical sceptical hypothesis, it follows that if one knows the everyday proposition, then one must know the denial of the radical sceptical hypothesis as well. So, for example, since having hands is manifestly inconsistent with being a (handless) BIV, if one knows that one has two hands, then one also knows that one is not a BIV. Finally, the third part of the response is the extraction of the anti-sceptical conclusion that one knows the denial of the target radical sceptical hypothesis, in this case that one is not a BIV.

Here, then, is a run-down of the argument, sticking to the BIV hypothesis throughout:

Mooreanism
(M1) I know that I have two hands.
(M2) If I know that I have two hands, then I know that I'm not a BIV.
(MC) I know that I'm not a BIV.

It is important to the Moorean view that there is nothing more to the stance than the presentation of an argument of this sort. The radical sceptic has called our knowledge into question, via the presentation of the radical sceptical hypothesis, and the Moorean, via his opposing argument, has rebutted the radical sceptic's claims. Thus, there is no case to answer, and hence nothing more that needs to be said. In this sense, then, the Moorean stance is a *pre-theoretical* proposal, in that it attempts to deal with the radical sceptical challenge in an entirely commonsense way which avoids the need for a theoretical response to the problem.

There are a number of problems with the Moorean strategy, but I will not be attempting to elucidate them all here.[4] Instead, I will just mention three key difficulties that the view faces.

Perhaps the most common complaint levelled at the Moorean argument is that there is something question-begging about responding to the radical sceptical problem in this way, in that it simply takes as an unquestioned premise in its argument the denial of the very claim that the radical sceptic will want to motivate as a conclusion of her argument. Call this the *dialectal impropriety* objection.[5]

We can get a grip on what the problem is here by considering the BIV-based radical sceptical argument formulated above. With this formulation of the radical sceptical argument and the Moorean argument set side-by-side, one can see that the debate here encapsulates that old philosophical chestnut that one philosopher's *modus ponens* is another philosopher's *modus tollens*. The second premise of both arguments—(BIV2) and (M2)—is exactly the same, and presumably the common motivation for both premises is the closure principle. But whereas the Moorean takes his everyday knowledge as secure and argues on this basis that he also has the required anti-sceptical knowledge, the radical sceptic begins by highlighting the implausibility of anti-sceptical knowledge and argues on this basis that we also lack everyday knowledge. With the debate so construed, however, one can see why the Moorean strategy can seem so dialectically inappropriate. The radical sceptic has given us an apparently compelling argument for thinking that we lack everyday knowledge. In response, the Moorean simply helps himself to the denial of the contested conclusion and reasons on this basis to the negation of the premise of the radical sceptical argument.

Given that the Moorean argument begins and ends with this strategy, it is little wonder that few find it persuasive. At the very least, some sort of diagnostic story needs to be offered by the Moorean to explain away the intuitive appeal of radical scepticism, since without such a story we seem to be passing the problem by. Part of this diagnostic story will inevitably involve an epistemological theory to back up the view—a theory which explains, for example, why we can know the denials of radical sceptical hypotheses after all, contrary to our first intuitions on this score.

A second, and related, difficulty with the Moorean response is that it seems to offer us, at most, a *draw* with the radical sceptic, rather than a resolution of the radical sceptical problem. After all, given that the radical sceptical argument is just the *modus tollens* to Moore's *modus ponens*, and since both arguments have intuitive premises, it appears that the dialectical situation is that we are faced with two opposing arguments of equal force. If this is right, then even despite the Moorean argument we still have just as much reason to be radical sceptics as to be Mooreans. Put another way, it is still the case even granted the Moorean proposal that we have no good reason *not* to be radical sceptics. This is a kind of second-order radical scepticism which, while not obviously reducible to its first-order cousin (which would hold that we have reason to be radical sceptics), is still enough to make Moorean anti-scepticism not nearly as intellectually satisfying as it might at first appear. Call this the *impasse* objection.[6]

Finally, a third key problem with Mooreanism is that the Moorean argument seems to consist of a series of assertions which strike one as conversationally inappropriate, if not just plain absurd or contentless. As a number of commentators have noted—most trenchantly Wittgenstein (1969) in his final notebooks—the assertions in question in the Moorean argument seem to offend against our usual usage of the term 'know'.[7] This phrase plays a very special role in our practices of knowledge self-ascription, but, crucially, not one that seems applicable to the kind of anti-sceptical assertions that the Moorean makes.

In particular, there appears to be something conversationally very odd about asserting that one knows the denial of a specific radical sceptical hypothesis. That is, even if one is willing to grant with the neo-Moorean that one can indeed know that one is not, say, a BIV, it still needs to be explained why any explicit claim to know that one is not a BIV (i.e., 'I know that I am not a BIV') sounds so conversationally inappropriate. Call this the *conversational impropriety* objection.

Although not an exhaustive list, these three objections do capture the heart of the difficulties facing Mooreanism, and thus highlight the work that a *neo*-Moorean view, one which can evade the problems facing Mooreanism, has to do.

§3. Contemporary Neo-Mooreanism

While few are persuaded by the Moorean anti-sceptical view, there are positions available in the literature which broadly mirror such a stance while differing on crucial details, positions that I have elsewhere termed 'neo-Moorean' (Pritchard 2002*b*, §8; cf. Pritchard 2002*c*). Like Mooreanism, neo-Mooreanism confronts the radical sceptical problem head-on by allowing that we can know the denials of radical sceptical hypotheses. Accordingly, again like Mooreanism, the view avoids radical scepticism while retaining the closure principle by denying the first premise in the radical sceptic's argument, (S1). Furthermore, neo-Mooreanism achieves this in a Moorean spirit by avoiding, as much as possible, epistemological revisionism.[8] Unlike Mooreanism, however, neo-Moorean views aim to offer the wider theoretical motivation for the proposal, thereby avoiding the kinds of problems facing Mooreanism just outlined. In this sense they are theoretical rather than pre-theoretical responses to the radical sceptical problem.

One of the key issues facing neo-Mooreanism is how to explain how we can know the denials of radical sceptical hypotheses. The standard line in this regard usually adverts to some form of the safety principle for knowledge, as defended, for example, by Ernest Sosa (1999). This principle holds, roughly, that what is essential to knowledge is that one has a belief that could not have easily been false. The basic idea is that provided sceptical error-possibilities are indeed far-fetched, then it follows that one's true belief that one is not a victim of such an error-possibility will be such that it couldn't have easily been false, and so can count as knowledge.

The underlying motivation for safety comes from the intuition that what is essential to knowledge is that it is non-lucky true belief, where the safety principle captures the heart of this anti-luck intuition. Thus, the claim is that provided that one's environment is epistemically friendly, then one's anti-sceptical beliefs will not be lucky and hence can count as instances of knowledge.[9]

Clearly, however, the neo-Moorean cannot leave the story there, since we still need to be told how the neo-Moorean stance can avoid the problems which we saw afflicting Mooreanism above. Moreover, we are also owed an explanation of the evidential basis of this anti-sceptical knowledge (or else an explanation of how it could feasibly lack an evidential basis). In order to begin filling in some of this detail it is essential that we first factor the epistemic externalism/internalism distinction into this discussion, since the nature of the further detail will be dependent upon which side of this contrast one stands.

It ought to be clear straight away that motivating a version of neo-Mooreanism along the standard epistemic internalist lines that we considered in part one (§6) is not going to be at all easy. We noted in part one that standard epistemic internalist proposals endorse either accessibilism or mentalism, along with being in addition committed to the new evil genius thesis. In order to keep our discussion here manageable, in what follows we will bracket the mentalist option and focus on the combination of accessibilism and the new evil genius thesis (i.e., henceforth, then, when we refer to the 'standard epistemic internalist' position we will have this kind of proposal in mind). As we saw in part one, such a view holds that the internalist epistemic support an agent has for their beliefs is constituted solely by facts that she can know by reflection alone, where the only facts that an agent can know by reflection alone are facts that the agent's recently envatted physical duplicate can also know by reflection alone. Once we factor this proposal into a theory of knowledge, we would have a view on which knowledge entails the possession of a significant degree of internalist epistemic support, where this is understood along the lines just set out.

It should be clear why the standard epistemic internalist account struggles to explain how we might know the denials of sceptical hypotheses. For if one's epistemic support is restricted to those reflectively accessible facts that one's envatted counterpart can also know by reflection alone, then it is hard to see how one could have reflective access to any facts which could indicate that one is not a BIV. In short, one has on this view no more reason for discounting the BIV hypothesis than a BIV has for discounting it, and on the face of it they have no reason for discounting it at all. The problem is thus that on this view the relevant belief seems to enjoy no internal epistemic support, and yet such support is required if the belief is to amount to knowledge. And, of course, if one cannot know that one is not a BIV, then with the closure principle in play one's knowledge of many everyday propositions, such as that one has two hands, is also under threat.

One can put this point into sharper relief by considering what the specifically evidential basis of our putative anti-sceptical knowledge would be on the standard epistemic internalist account. Consider again the favouring principle that we put forward in part two (§3):

The Favouring Principle
If S (i) knows that φ, and (ii) knows that ψ, and (iii) knows that φ entails ψ, then S has better evidence in support of her belief that φ than for believing that not-ψ.

In essence, this principle demands that one's knowledge be evidentially supported, where evidential support here means support which favours what is believed over known to be incompatible alternatives (that is, which provides more support for what is believed than it does for the known to be incompatible alternatives). So construed, the principle seems entirely uncontentious, since it is hard to see how one's evidence could be genuinely supporting evidence if it did not perform this 'favouring' function.

The trouble is, however, that once one feeds radical sceptical hypotheses into this principle in the context of the standard epistemic internalist account, then one immediately generates the radical sceptical problem. Think, for example, of your belief that you are not a BIV. Clearly, one knows that being a BIV is inconsistent with not being a BIV. With the favouring principle in play, then, it follows on the standard epistemic internalist account that knowing that one is not a BIV requires one to possess reflectively accessible evidence which favours one's not being a BIV over being a BIV. But given that the standard form of epistemic internalism also subscribes to the new evil genius thesis an obvious problem now emerges. For it now follows that the facts which are accessible to one are only those facts which are also accessible to one's envatted counterpart. But how then can one have reflectively accessible evidence which possibly favours one's not being a BIV over being a BIV?

By the same token, one cannot know that one has, say, two hands, either. Given the favouring principle, in order to know that one has two hands one needs to have evidence which favours this belief over the known to be incompatible alternative that one is a BIV. But if the facts which are accessible to one are only those facts which are also accessible to one's envatted counterpart, then how could one possibly have any reflectively accessible evidence which could play this favouring role? Hence, one cannot know that one has two hands, and much else besides.[10,11]

It is unsurprising, then, that there are relatively few neo-Moorean stances in the literature that are conceived along standard epistemic internalist lines.[12] Epistemic externalism, on the other hand, is clearly on stronger ground when it comes to motivating a neo-Moorean position. After all, that one lacks adequate reflectively accessible grounds by standard epistemic internalist lights for believing that one is not a BIV will not on this view decide the issue of whether or not one can have knowledge of this proposition, since other factors, such as the reliability of the process through which one formed one's belief, can also be relevant. Since it is a general feature of epistemic externalism that it allows that knowledge can sometimes be possessed even in the absence of adequate reflectively accessible grounds, this line of argument is entirely in keeping with their broader position.

Indeed, the epistemic externalist can use this point to diagnose why (S1) in the radical sceptical argument, while intuitive, must be rejected. Epistemic externalism is independently motivated, after all, and yet the motivation for (S1) could plausibly be claimed to derive from an implicit commitment to epistemic internalism. That is, the thinking behind this premise could well be characterized as being that since we lack good reflectively accessible grounds for our beliefs in the denials of radical sceptical hypotheses, we lack knowledge of these propositions. But this is an entailment that only goes through by standard epistemic internalist lights, and hence it can be resisted by the epistemic externalist.

Moreover, notice that the fact that the standard form of epistemic internalism faces such an uphill struggle when it comes to dealing with the problem of radical scepticism is also a point in favour of epistemic externalist neo-Mooreanism. For the proponent of this view can reasonably argue that the failure of this alternative proposal to deal with radical scepticism means that they are the only game in town (remember that proponents of both epistemic externalism and standard forms of epistemic internalism regard epistemological disjunctivism as a position that is simply unavailable). This, then, becomes for the epistemic externalist one more reason for preferring their account over their internalist rival.

As with other neo-Moorean views, since epistemic externalist neo-Mooreanism holds that we can know the denials of radical sceptical hypotheses, so there is no reason on this score for it to reject the closure principle. Moreover, provided that 'evidence' is interpreted in a sufficiently broad way so that it extends beyond one's reflectively accessible rational support—as presumably it would be interpreted by an epistemic externalist—then it seems that the epistemic externalist neo-Moorean could plausibly argue that their view is compatible with the favouring principle too. After all, on such a broad conception of evidence it ought to be possible to have better evidence for believing everyday propositions than to believe sceptical alternatives.[13,14]

Taking the epistemic externalist route out of the radical sceptical problem is not without its own difficulties, however, since there clearly is a strong intuitive pull towards seeking a resolution of this problem along epistemic internalist lines.[15] Indeed, I take it that it is most natural to think of the radical sceptical challenge as specifically asking us to offer an appropriate rational basis for our everyday beliefs, given the existence of radial sceptical hypotheses which, it seems, we have no adequate rational basis for thinking are false. So construed, the radical sceptical challenge is not met head-on by an epistemic externalist version of neo-Mooreanism at all. Instead, it rather side-steps this challenge by offering an independent basis for rejecting epistemic internalism. That is, what we seek in response to the radical sceptical problem is *rationally grounded* anti-sceptical knowledge, but what epistemic externalist neo-Mooreanism offers us is a basis for rejecting the idea that all *bona fide* knowledge must be rationally grounded, coupled with an explanation, cast along specifically epistemic externalist lines, of how we can have the anti-sceptical knowledge in question (albeit without the accompanying rational grounds).

If it were true that there is no way of rendering the neo-Moorean anti-sceptical strategy along epistemic internalist lines, then I think this drawback in the epistemic externalist neo-Moorean approach would be something that the epistemic externalist could quite legitimately respond to with a shrug of the shoulders. As noted above, that the epistemic externalist neo-Moorean account doesn't face the kind of formidable challenges that confront standard epistemic internalist neo-Moorean views can be taken as further reason for thinking that it is epistemic internalism which is the joker in the pack here. That is, the fact that the most natural way to characterize the 'core' radical sceptical problem is along specifically epistemic internalist lines—even though such a view seems completely unable to deal with this problem—can be utilized by the epistemic externalist neo-Moorean as a reason for thinking that this is a problem which *ought* to be side-stepped with an externalist epistemic resolution.

Of course, the foregoing discussion effectively takes for granted—in line with current thinking in contemporary epistemology—that the only kinds of neo-Moorean views available are either cast along epistemic externalist lines or standard epistemic internalist lines. But epistemological disjunctivism has the potential to be a game-changer on this score. We have already seen in parts one and two that this is a view which doesn't face the kind of obvious problems that can be levelled at it, and thus that it is a 'live' theoretical proposal. The challenge now is to see if this view can be successfully applied to the problem of radical scepticism. In particular, can epistemological disjunctivism offer us a way of resolving this problem that is cast along epistemic internalist lines, but which lacks the formidable drawbacks associated with standard epistemic internalist responses to radical scepticism? I will be suggesting that it can.

§4. A Simpleminded Epistemological Disjunctivist Neo-Mooreanism

As we will see, when applied to the problem of radical scepticism, epistemological disjunctivism offers a unique style of neo-Mooreanism.[16] We can set out such a view by focusing on the usual pair of cases, albeit re-characterized in terms of the taxonomy of good and bad cases outlined in part one. We thus have a good+ case in which the agent is in a scenario which is both subjectively and objectively epistemically good, and a corresponding introspectively indistinguishable bad++ case in which the agent is a BIV (where in the latter case the agent's perception is non-veridical and the environment is objectively epistemically bad).

Given our remarks about good+ and bad++ cases in part two, a simpleminded way of responding to radical scepticism on epistemological disjunctivist grounds becomes available which merely extends the reasoning in the Zula case to this problem. We also indicated in part two, however, that there is a fundamental difficulty which afflicts such a crude attempt to deal with radical scepticism, and it is worthwhile reminding ourselves of this problem.

Here is the simpleminded form of epistemological disjunctivist neo-Mooreanism in question. In the good+ case our agent—let's call him 'John'—perceptually knows the target empirical proposition which entails that he is not a BIV (let's call this proposition p), where sufficient epistemic support for this knowledge is provided by the relevant reflectively accessible factive reason (i.e., his seeing that p). Like Zula, John does not need to take a view on whether he is a BIV in order to know that p (nor does it matter that he is unable to perceptually discriminate between the objects at issue in the two scenarios—hands and 'vat-hands', say). If, however, he is confronted with this hypothesis, then he needs to take a view on it and so either have an adequate epistemic basis for believing that not-BIV, or else no longer believe (and hence know) that p (and much else besides). But on the simpleminded view such epistemic support for believing that not-BIV is easy to come by, since John has reflectively available to him rational support for his belief that p which (he is fully aware) *entails p* and hence which entails not-BIV as well. Hence, by undertaking the relevant competent deduction he can come to know on this reflective basis that he is not a BIV.[17]

Expressed in the terminology introduced in part two, what is being suggested here is that although John cannot perceptually discriminate between the (objects at issue in the) good+ case that he is in and the corresponding bad++ BIV scenario, nor distinguish these two scenarios by introspection alone, he can nonetheless *reflectively* distinguish between them (i.e., he can distinguish them by dint of the combined use of introspection and a priori reasoning). There is thus a sense in which John can know that he is not a BIV, and know this in virtue of reflectively accessible rational support. We thus have a neo-Moorean response that is cast along epistemic internalist lines which, in virtue of delivering the requisite internalist epistemic support for our beliefs in the denials of radical sceptical hypotheses, can avoid the problems levelled at standard epistemic internalist renderings of neo-Mooreanism noted above.

We noted in part two that there is a big problem facing this kind of simpleminded epistemological disjunctivist response to scepticism. For there is a crucial difference between the kind of bad++ case at issue in our discussion of Zula, and the sort of bad++ case put forward by the radical sceptic. In particular, the sceptical bad++ case by its nature calls the rational basis for the agent's beliefs into question *en masse*, in contrast to the error-possibility in play in the Zula example which is specific to the particular perceptual belief that she is forming. So, for example, Zula can appeal to independent grounds in support of her belief that what she is looking at is not a cleverly disguised mule, grounds which are not already called into question by the cleverly disguised mule hypothesis in play. In contrast, the radical sceptical hypothesis that you are a BIV calls into question whatever other grounds you might have in support of your ordinary perceptual beliefs as well, and so an 'independent' rational basis is in this context unavailable.

The problem is thus that while Zula can come to know that what she is looking at is a zebra rather than a cleverly disguised mule by appealing only to favouring grounds (i.e., even though she lacks the relevant perceptual discriminatory capacities), this is because she is in a position to appeal to independent epistemic support (i.e., grounds which are not themselves called into question by the target error-possibility). But since independent epistemic support of this sort is unavailable in the radical sceptical case, it seems that the epistemological disjunctivist is not in a position to exploit favouring epistemic support in order to motivate a parallel strategy to resolve the radical sceptical challenge.

This does not mean that the epistemological disjunctivist cannot respond to the radical sceptical problem, however. Instead, what it shows is that we need a more complicated story about how the reflectively accessible factive rational support that the agent has in the good+ case can be employed in a competent deduction such that it provides adequate reflectively accessible rational support for the agent's belief that she is not a victim of a sceptical bad++ case. As we will see, even once we do this, further problems will arise. For if we do have reflectively accessible factive rational support for our beliefs in the denials of radical sceptical hypotheses, then why does it seem inappropriate to outright claim to know these propositions? Relatedly, why do we have such a strong conviction that such propositions cannot be known? We will return to such problems in due course, but first let us consider the more immediate issue of how to adapt the simpleminded epistemological disjunctivist response to radical scepticism so that it becomes a plausible candidate view in this regard.[18]

§5. Motivating Epistemological Disjunctivist Neo-Mooreanism

Recall our discussion of the Zula case in part two (§§6–7) where we examined ways in which Zula should respond to the cleverly disguised mule hypothesis by the lights of the two-tiered relevant alternatives view that we put forward. We noted that it can make an important difference whether this error-possibility is epistemically motivated rather than merely raised. In particular, the epistemic bar required for ruling out this error-possibility can be in part determined by whether the error-possibility has been epistemically grounded. And recall that we needed to consider how the epistemological disjunctivist proposal functioned in terms of a two-tiered relevant alternatives theory in order to see this difference, since on standard views it didn't emerge.

On standard views, it didn't matter whether the error-possibility in question was epistemically motivated or merely raised. If, for example, Zula's rational basis for believing that p is that it seems to her as if p, then clearly this won't suffice to allow her to conclude that the relevant bad++ case does not obtain, since it would just as much seem to her as if p in that case too. And this applies even if the target error-possibility is merely raised.

In contrast, on the epistemological disjunctivist view if the error-possibility has not been epistemically motivated but merely raised, then Zula *doesn't* need to appeal to independent rational grounds in support of her belief (this is only required if it is epistemically motivated). The reason for this is that because her reflectively accessible rational basis for this belief is factive this itself suffices to directly exclude the target error-possibility. Given that this error-possibility is epistemically unmotivated, there is thus no bar to her rejecting this error-possibility simply by appealing to this factive rational basis. That is, if the reflectively accessible rational support available to Zula is that she sees that *p*, and she is presented with an unmotivated error-possibility (a bad++ case) that is inconsistent with *p*, then she is entitled to appeal to this rational support to dismiss that error-possibility.

Clearly, however, if the error-possibility *is* adequately epistemically grounded then, as we noted in part two (§7), it would not be appropriate for the agent to undertake the relevant competent deduction to exclude the bad++ case, even where the rational basis available to one is factive. If one is offered sufficient grounds for supposing that one does not see that *p*, but merely seems to see that *p*, then one cannot legitimately appeal to the fact that one (putatively) sees that *p* in response to this challenge. Instead, independent grounds must be sought which can neutralize these grounds for doubt.

As noted above, however, the problem in the radical sceptical case is that it is far from clear where such independent grounds could come from. In the Zula case, the agent was able to appeal to background considerations which weren't themselves being called into question by the error-possibility in play. In contrast, whatever relevant background considerations that John possesses—e.g., grounds for thinking that the BIV error-possibility is unlikely, given the state of current technology—will be themselves called into question by this error-possibility.

Crucially, however, radical sceptical error-possibilities are never epistemically motivated but are instead only merely raised. Consider the BIV-based radical sceptical argument that we formulated above (§1). The claim is not that there are empirical grounds for supposing the BIV hypothesis to be true, but just that we are unable to know that it is false—i.e., (BIV1)—and that we need to know that it is false if we are to have the kind of everyday knowledge that we typically attribute to ourselves—i.e., (BIV2). A radical sceptical argument which offered empirical grounds in support of the target radical sceptical hypothesis would thus constitute a very different way of arguing for radical scepticism.

Moreover, a radical sceptical argument which incorporated this feature would be problematic in ways that the style of radical sceptical argument which we are focusing on is not. In the first instance, the problem is that the very idea of there being empirical grounds for thinking that we are the victims of a radical sceptical scenario is itself problematic. Consider, for example, the kind of epistemic support that one might offer in support of the claim that we are BIVs. Suppose, for instance, that one receives testimony from otherwise reliable testifiers to the effect that one is a BIV. The problem is, of course, that if one is a BIV then one's informants are no more real than one's non-existent hands. But then why should their testimony carry any epistemic weight? The point in play here is an entirely general one of course. Because it is in the very nature of radical sceptical hypotheses that they call one's empirical beliefs into question *en masse*, it is therefore inevitable that they will call into question whatever empirical basis one takes oneself to have for supposing such a hypothesis to be true. It is thus no wonder that the radical sceptical challenge avoids incorporating commitments of this sort.

There is also a further reason why the radical sceptical challenge does not incorporate such empirical claims, and this is that to do so would require the sceptic to take on empirical commitments of their own, and the sceptic—if she is doing her job properly anyway—simply isn't in the business of doing that. In order to understand this point, we first need to realize that radical scepticism, properly construed, is not a *position* at all (i.e., a theoretical proposal that someone defends), but is rather meant to be a *paradox* (i.e., a series of highly intuitive but logically inconsistent claims).[19]

We can recast the BIV-based radical sceptical argument we presented above in the form of paradox as follows:

BIV-Based Radical Scepticism qua *Paradox*
(BIV1) I don't know that I'm not a BIV.
(BIV2) If I know that I have two hands, then I know that I'm not a BIV.
(BIV3) I do know that I have two hands.

All we have done here is negate the conclusion of the BIV-based radical sceptical argument, (BIVC). What we now have are three highly intuitive claims which are jointly inconsistent.[20] Thus, we have to deny one of these claims, but whichever one we reject this denial will be counterintuitive.

We are now in a position to distinguish between radical scepticism *qua* position and radical scepticism *qua* paradox. The latter consists simply in the demonstration that there is this deep and fundamental tension within our own epistemological concepts, as exemplified by the three claims just set out. As the proponent of a paradox the radical sceptic is (they claim) not putting forward any theses themselves at all, but rather merely highlighting this fundamental problem regarding our own intuitive epistemological commitments. In contrast, as the proponent of a position the radical sceptic is endorsing at least one specific thesis, in that they are responding to the radical sceptical paradox by affirming the denial of the third intuitive claim made above—i.e., (BIV3).

Notice that viewing radical scepticism as a paradox rather than a position alters the dialectical situation when it comes to dealing with the radical sceptical problem quite considerably. Dealing with the radical sceptical *position* is far easier than dealing with the radical sceptical *paradox* since the former requires a proponent who has commitments of her own and, in particular, who needs to make her position stable and internally consistent, which is not an easy thing for a radical sceptic to do.[21] In outlining the radical sceptical paradox, however, one doesn't need to worry about any of this, since one is not putting forward a view at all; rather, one is simply demonstrating that there is an inherent tension within our own epistemological concepts.

With the foregoing in mind, it should be clear that any form of radical scepticism that incorporates an appeal to empirical grounds in support of radical sceptical hypotheses would inevitably be drawn down the road of offering their scepticism as a position rather than a paradox. This is because it is in the very nature of radical scepticism *qua* paradox that it is meant to be simply extracting deep tensions within our own commitments, rather than being in the business of putting forward commitments of its own.

Moreover, notice that even when radical scepticism is offered *qua* position rather than *qua* paradox, it is still the case that the sceptic concerned will usually have the good sense to eschew *empirical* commitments. A radical sceptic who endorses the denial of (BIV3) does so, I take it, because she maintains, on purely a priori grounds, that this is the best way of responding to this trilemma. There is no appeal to empirical claims here, and thus the problem regarding a possible radical sceptical appeal to empirical claims that we noted above—in a nutshell, that they are effectively self-undermining—does not arise. In contrast, a form of radical scepticism *qua* position which incorporates empirical commitments of its own has to in addition deal with these further problems.

It should thus come as no surprise that radical sceptical hypotheses are always merely raised and never epistemically motivated by appeal to empirical considerations. As we have seen, such appeals would be self-defeating and would in any case undermine the plausibility of the radical sceptical argument at issue. But with this point in play, it follows that Zula *can* appeal to the factive reflectively accessible rational support available to her in order to dismiss the radical sceptical scenario in play.

What is missing from the simpleminded version of epistemological disjunctivist neo-Mooreanism is thus an account of why the extent to which one needs to cite an independent rational basis in order to dismiss an error-possibility can be dependent on whether the error-possibility has been epistemically motivated. We have seen that in cases—whether sceptical or non-sceptical—where an agent has factive rational support available to her, she needs an independent rational basis to dismiss the target error-possibility (which is inconsistent with this rational basis) *only* where that error-possibility has been epistemically motivated. We have also seen, however, that radical sceptical error-possibilities are in their nature lacking in epistemic motivation. The net result is that epistemological disjunctivists are able to appeal to the factive reflectively accessible that is available to them in the good+ case in order to motivate a form of neo-Mooreanism after all, so long as they supply this additional account of why independent grounds for dismissing the target error-possibility are not required in this case.

I do not for one minute doubt that many will find this puzzling. That is, I grant that it does seem *prima facie* odd to claim, in the context of a radical sceptical hypothesis like the BIV hypothesis, that since one has reflective access to factive rational support which entails the falsity of this hypothesis, and since no one has offered an empirical basis for thinking the BIV hypothesis true, so one can conclude, employing only a priori reasoning, that one is rationally entitled to dismiss the BIV hypothesis (i.e., and thereby know it to be false). But I think that the sources of this disquiet have been one-by-one neutralized.

For example, one source of concern might be the idea that one can have a reflective route to such a specific empirical conclusion. This concern would be a version of the access problem that we examined, and dealt with, in part one (§7). As we saw there, there is nothing disturbing about this conclusion once we make explicit that the claim is only that, in the good+ case, agents are able to reflectively 'extract' from their *empirical* factive reflectively accessible support certain empirical consequences (in this instance, that they are not in the bad++ case).

A second source of concern might be the idea that since one cannot perceptually discriminate between (the target objects in) a good+ case and a corresponding bad++ case (like the BIV case), so one ought not to be able to know that one is in a good+ case rather than a corresponding bad++ case. But we have seen that this line of thinking is predicated on a mistake too. As we saw in part two (§4), even if we set epistemological disjunctivism to one side, it remains true that an agent who cannot perceptually discriminate between (the target objects in) a good+ case and a corresponding bad++ case can nonetheless have adequate *favouring* epistemic support for believing that the first case obtains rather than the second (and thereby know that the first case obtains rather than the second).

A third source of concern has been discussed in some detail in this section—*viz.*, that the appeal to favouring epistemic support only works in cases where one has an independent epistemic basis for dismissing the target error-possibility, something that is lacking when it comes to radical scepticism. But we have seen that this concern is misplaced too, once we recognize that if we have a reflectively accessible *factive* rational basis for our beliefs, then we do not need independent grounds to dismiss *ungrounded* error-possibilities which are inconsistent with this rational support. Moreover, we have also shown that radical sceptical error-possibilities are indeed by their nature epistemically ungrounded.

With these points in mind, I think the natural residual resistance to a response to radical scepticism that is cast along epistemological disjunctivist lines should be re-evaluated. This is not to say that we are home and dry, however, since there are further issues that this view needs to address, not least the awkwardness of making the relevant Moorean assertions. (For on this view one possesses factive reflectively accessible grounds in support of the target assertions. So what could possibly be amiss with asserting them? This could thus be thought of being a fourth source of concern when it comes to epistemological disjunctivist neo-Mooreanism.)

First though, we need to explore further the kind of neo-Moorean anti-sceptical proposal that epistemological disjunctivism makes available to us. As we will see, this will enable us to further motivate the position.

§6. Overriding versus Undercutting Anti-Sceptical Strategies

In the last section we noted the distinction between thinking of the radical sceptical challenge as a position and as a paradox, and we offered the following formulation of the radical sceptical paradox, at least insofar as it made use of the BIV sceptical hypothesis:

BIV-Based Radical Scepticism qua *Paradox*
(BIV1) I don't know that I'm not a BIV.
(BIV2) If I know that I have two hands, then I know that I'm not a BIV.
(BIV3) I do know that I have two hands.

We also noted that radical scepticism *qua* position is the view that (BIV3) has to go. On the face of it, this is the least appealing of the three options, and it is important to understand why. The explanation is that (BIV3) is different from the other two claims that make up this paradox in that it simply reflects a commonsense conviction that one can recognize as intuitive even before one engages in philosophical reflection. Pre-philosophically we all take ourselves to have widespread knowledge of the world around us, and hence we take ourselves to have knowledge in paradigm cases like the one under consideration.

In contrast, (BIV1) and (BIV2) are claims which we are led to see are intuitive by engaging in philosophical reflection.[22] Pre-philosophically, we don't even consider radical sceptical error-possibilities after all, and certainly not the epistemic principles which connect the epistemic standing of our everyday beliefs with our (proto-) beliefs in the denials of radical sceptical hypotheses. This means that we have a choice between on the one hand allowing radical scepticism and rejecting commonsense, or else on the other hand preserving commonsense by denying one (or both) of the philosophically intuitive claims, (BIV1) and (BIV2). Those who deny the closure principle deny (BIV2), and we have already noted that this is not a very attractive resolution to the problem. That leaves neo-Mooreanism of some form, the defining characteristic of which is that it rejects (BIV1).

But even though the radical sceptical resolution of this paradox (i.e., where radical scepticism is construed as a position) is problematic, this doesn't mean that the remaining anti-sceptical resolutions to this paradox are thereby intellectually satisfying. For responding to any paradox by denying an intuition, whether one that is pre-theoretical like (BIV3), or one that we are led to on reflection of our epistemic practices and concepts (like (BIV1) and (BIV2)), is not going to be very intellectually satisfying. Indeed, it seems to simply reaffirm the original sceptical paradox—i.e., that there is this deep and fundamental tension within our epistemological concepts. And beating the radical sceptic—i.e., radical scepticism *qua* position—is of little use to us if it leaves the radical sceptical paradox intact.

So what would constitute an intellectually satisfying response to this paradox? To consider this question we first need to notice that there is more than one way in which one might go about rejecting an intuitive claim that forms part of a paradox. Clearly, as just noted, to simply reject one of the claims that make up the paradox without offering any account as to what warrants such a rejection would not be an intellectually satisfying way of responding to the sceptical paradox, but then no serious anti-sceptical strategy would take this route (though perhaps Mooreanism, read uncharitably anyway, might be applicable here). Even so, we can distinguish between two ways in which anti-sceptical proposals might motivate their rejection of the relevant intuitive claim.

On the one hand, one might *override* the target claim by conceding that despite its intuitiveness there are independent theoretical grounds for rejecting it (intuitions are defeasible guides to the truth, after all). On the other hand, one might *undercut* the target claim by showing that it is not intuitive at all, once properly understood. If one presents an undercutting strategy then one is in effect arguing that what looked like a paradox was not in fact a paradox after all. In contrast, in presenting an overriding strategy one is in effect conceding that one is faced with a genuine paradox—in the broad sense outlined above involving a logical clash of intuitive claims—it is just that there is a sound theoretical basis on which we can reject one of these claims and thereby evade this paradox.[23]

Of course, there are going to be penumbral cases where it isn't at all clear which type of anti-sceptical proposal is in play. After all, an overriding anti-sceptical proposal that offers a very compelling theoretical story about why we should reject the target claim will inevitably be hard to distinguish from an undercutting proposal. Still, the distinction is clear enough. What is interesting about this distinction for our purposes is that undercutting anti-sceptical proposals are clearly preferable to overriding ones. For what we seek in an intellectually satisfying response to the radical sceptical paradox is ideally a proposal that removes the intellectual crisis prompted by the paradox, and that is only really achieved by an under-cutting strategy. If the claims that led to the paradox remain with their intuitive force intact, however, then the philosophical pull of scepticism will continue even after we have adopted the relevant anti-sceptical stance.

Indeed, overriding anti-sceptical proposals are inherently in danger of *accentuating* rather than resolving the radical sceptical problem, since if one holds that the only way to avoid the paradox is to adopt a certain theoreti-cal position which leaves the intuitive force of the paradox still standing, then that commits one to a kind of intellectual bad faith. On the one hand, one is rationally committed to holding the relevant theoretical position. But, on the other hand, one is also still in the grip of the relevant intuitions which led to the paradox. The original paradox is thus now accompanied by a kind of *quasi*-meta-paradox.

The dialectical problem facing epistemic externalist versions of neo-Mooreanism is that they are by their nature overriding anti-sceptical proposals, and thus are to this extent problematic. The epistemic extern-alist is not disputing that intuition supports (BIV1), it is just that they claim that this intuition reflects a misplaced commitment to epistemic internal-ism and hence should be overridden by the independent theoretical considerations which, they claim, favour epistemic externalism. But this means, of course, that the original tension in our epistemic concepts highlighted by the radical sceptical paradox remains, albeit with its force partially blunted. We are thus bound to feel some intellectual unease with such an approach.

In particular, one will naturally feel that this response to the radical sceptical problem only succeeds to the extent that it shifts the goalposts. For it seems that what this epistemic externalist response to the radical sceptical paradox highlights is that this problem is not targeted at our putative widespread possession of knowledge *simpliciter* at all, but is rather specifically concerned with our putative widespread possession of knowledge which is adequately supported by reflectively accessible grounds.

If the epistemic externalist brand of neo-Mooreanism were the only anti-sceptical game in town, then one might be able to live with this problem (it is certainly far from fatal). Crucially, however, there is an epistemic internalist brand of neo-Mooreanism available which, by offering a non-standard version of epistemic internalism cast along epistemological disjunctivist lines, can deliver an undercutting anti-sceptical proposal. For notice that what is distinctive about this strategy when compared with epistemic externalist and classical epistemic internalist versions of neo-Mooreanism is that it can allow that our knowledge of the denials of rational sceptical hypotheses *is* rationally supported, and hence it can meet the radical sceptical problem head-on. In particular, the radical sceptic can't appeal to our lack of adequate reflectively accessible reasons for believing the denials of radical sceptical hypotheses as a means of promoting the intuition that we lack knowledge of these propositions.

There is another aspect of this anti-sceptical proposal which is also crucial to determining its dialectical credentials. For recall that we argued in part one (§2) that epistemological disjunctivism could stake a claim to being the natural account of (paradigmatic) perceptual knowledge that one would offer prior to engaging in philosophical reflection. That is, in our ordinary language we talk as if paradigm cases of perceptual knowledge are indeed supported by factive reflectively accessible reasons of the relevant type. The problem is that philosophical reflection tends to generate a certain picture of the possible ways in which a plausible account of perceptual knowledge might be forged, a picture which excludes epistemological disjunctivism. In contrast, we have argued that once epistemological disjunctivism is properly developed and its supposed problems examined and neutralized, then it becomes apparent that it is a viable proposal after all, one that has many key attractions for epistemologists.

This facet of the epistemological disjunctivist proposal is important when it comes to its dialectical credentials in the radical sceptical debate, because it sides the proposal with commonsense against theory. More specifically, the radical sceptical problem is on this view the product of misplaced theory rather than intuition, and hence the paradox simply doesn't arise. We noted above that the intuitions in play with regard to (BIV1) and (BIV2) in the radical sceptical paradox are not part of commonsense, but are rather the result of philosophical reflection. This generates an opening for those who wish to undercut the radical sceptical paradox by arguing that it in fact arises out of misplaced theory rather than commonsense (such an opening is not available to the radical sceptic, *qua* proponent of a position, of course, since they *do* deny a commonsense intuition).

This is certainly the case when it comes to epistemological disjunctivism, since this has a story to tell about how the commonsense picture of our rational standing with regard to perceptual beliefs can be as it is usually supposed, and with this story in play it follows that the intuition driving (BIV1) is misplaced. That is, on this view we are led away from the natural picture on which we can have factive reflectively accessible support for our beliefs in paradigm cases of perceptual knowledge by faulty philosophical reasoning. Once that reasoning is blocked, and the natural—epistemological disjunctivist—picture is restored, then one is in a position to argue that the intuitions which drive claims like (BIV1) should be rejected out of hand.

So epistemological disjunctivist neo-Mooreanism represents an undercutting anti-sceptical strategy, and as such it is in a position to offer an intellectually satisfying response to the radical sceptical paradox. Indeed, if the epistemological disjunctivist is right that this putative paradox is actually at root motivated by faulty philosophical theory rather than by intuition, then the net effect of this anti-sceptical strategy is that radical scepticism is not the paradox that it claims to be. As such, this anti-sceptical proposal is much better placed to deal with the sceptical problem than its epistemic externalist neo-Moorean rival, who is committed to offering a dialectically weaker overriding anti-sceptical strategy.[24]

§7. Radical Scepticism and Quietism

Although there are some important similarities, this particular undercutting way of responding to the radical sceptical problem is ultimately significantly different from a *quietistic* response to this problem that is often associated with epistemological disjunctivism, and this is a good juncture to explore what these differences are. John McDowell is the obvious case in point in this respect, since while he advances a form of epistemological disjunctivism that is very similar to that defended here, and while he also thinks that this proposal in a sense resolves the problem of radical scepticism, he is quite clear that he does not think of the view as offering a direct response to this problem in the way that we have set out.

In particular, he does not conceive of the position he offers as issuing in an anti-sceptical *argument*, such as a neo-Moorean argument, which opposes, and thereby neutralizes, a specific radical sceptical argument, such as the argument we outlined above. Indeed, he is uncomfortable with the very idea of calling his treatment of scepticism an 'answer' to the problem at all, remarking, for example, that his view is "not well cast as an answer to skeptical challenges; it is more like a justification of a refusal to bother with them" (McDowell 1995, 888). This coyness is odd, since if McDowell's view—which shares the same general contours of the proposal set out here—is correct, then one *can* directly answer the sceptical challenge, and it is puzzling why McDowell doesn't recognize this.

Part of the reason why McDowell expresses his anti-scepticism in this cautious fashion is arguably because he regards such caution as being mandated by his avowedly 'diagnostic' treatment of the radical sceptical problem, where the diagnosis is that radical scepticism of the sort that he is interested in "expresses an inability to make sense of the idea of direct perceptual access to objective facts about the environment" (McDowell

2008, 378). Indeed, he makes this contrast between answering the radical sceptical problem and merely diagnosing it explicit in the following passage: "the thing to do is not to answer the skeptic's challenges, but to diagnose their seeming urgency as deriving from a misguided interiorization of reason" (McDowell 1995, 890). Still, it is far from obvious why a diagnosis of radical scepticism could not also be (and ought to be) an answer to the radical sceptical problem.

It is worthwhile in this regard to distinguish between a quietistic and non-quietistic version of an undercutting anti-sceptical strategy. What they both share is the idea that the radical sceptical problem is the result of faulty philosophizing, rather than being the natural intuitive puzzle that it appears to be. Where the quietistic undercutting anti-sceptical strategy parts company from its non-quietistic counterpart is in the claim that once we have exposed that the apparently visceral intuitive pull of radical scepticism is in fact the product of faulty philosophical theory, then there is nothing further of substance that needs to be said. Indeed, nothing could usefully be said, since that would be to take a route back into the very philosophical theorizing which generated the radical sceptical problem in the first place. In particular, there is nothing to be gained (on an anti-sceptical score at least) by offering an explanation of how we might have the contested knowledge of the denials of radical sceptical hypotheses. The point is that the radical sceptic has failed to show that we lack such knowledge, and thus failed to demonstrate that we lack the everyday knowledge that we take ourselves to have. Consequently, we can henceforth ignore the radical sceptical puzzle with impunity.

In contrast, a non-quietistic undercutting anti-sceptical strategy attempts to answer the sceptical problem head-on by providing the wider epistemological story which can account for how we can know the denials of sceptical hypotheses. Epistemological disjunctivist neo-Mooreanism, as I have described the position anyway, clearly falls into the non-quietist camp of undercutting proposals. McDowell's anti-sceptical stance, in comparison, is clearly in the quietistic camp of undercutting proposals.

The problem, however, is that since we have shown that a non-quietistic version of an undercutting anti-sceptical proposal is available—one that offers the supporting epistemology to explain how, contrary to first appearances, one could have the contested knowledge of the denials of radical sceptical hypotheses after all—it is hard to see why one would opt for the quietistic approach. Put simply, why walk away from the fray at the very moment that the radical sceptic has been deprived of her power? Why not finish the job while she is on the ropes?

Of course, part of the reason why McDowell is inclined towards a quietistic response to the radical sceptical problem is probably because he is persuaded by the merits of a more general philosophical quietism. In a nutshell, this wider quietism holds that the job of philosophers is not to argue one's way out of philosophical problems, but only to show that they are illusory problems in the first place, the product of philosophical theorizing. Since it was philosophical theorizing that generated the original problem, one is on a hiding to nothing in trying to use such theorizing to extricate oneself from a philosophical problem. Whether it is true that McDowell is wedded to such a conception of the philosophical project, this wider rationale for quietism is clearly not something that I can usefully engage with here.[25]

I want to suggest that even if it is true that such a wider quietism is substantially motivating McDowell's approach to scepticism, there is also a further reason, perhaps a subsidiary one, why quietism might be thought to be the right way to deal with the sceptical problem. Put another way, even if one does not buy into the idea of a general philosophical quietism, one might still think that in the radical sceptical case at least, a quietistic undercutting response is the way to go.

The reason for this is that it would seem that a non-quietistic undercutting response to the radical sceptical problem is in some sense committed to putting forward the very Moorean-style assertions which we noted above (§2) are clearly problematic. That is, a non-quietistic answer to the radical sceptic will, it seems, be committed to claiming, for example, that one knows the denials of radical sceptical hypotheses (and, more specifically, be committed to claiming that one knows these propositions because one knows everyday propositions and the relevant entailment). We noted earlier the awkwardness of such 'Moorean' assertions. Their awkwardness might well explain why someone like McDowell, regardless of his more general predilection towards quietism as a response to the perennial philosophical problems, prefers to simply remove the urgency from radical sceptical arguments and then refuse to engage with them thereafter, since it avoids the need to make assertions of this very sort.

In order to see this point in more detail, it is worthwhile considering how epistemic externalist and epistemic internalist neo-Moorean views would go about accounting for the impropriety of Moorean assertions. To begin with, note that, ordinarily at least, if one is to properly make an assertion, then one needs good reflectively accessible grounds to back up that assertion, especially if the assertion involves a claim to know. It would certainly be deemed inappropriate to unqualifiedly assert that p (much less 'I know that p'), thereby representing oneself as knowing that p, when one lacks good reflectively accessible grounds in support of this assertion. This means that the conditions under which it is appropriate to claim knowledge and the conditions under which knowledge is possessed will be closely connected on the epistemic internalist account, since they will tend to vary in line with whether one has reflectively accessible grounds in support of the target proposition.

In contrast, on the epistemic externalist account which allows that knowledge might be possessed even in the absence of good reflectively accessible grounds, there will be a class of cases in which agents have knowledge but cannot properly claim that knowledge because they lack adequate reflectively accessible supporting grounds for their claim. Think, for example, of the famous (and almost certainly apocryphal) chicken sexer case. As the story goes, this is an agent who is forming beliefs about the sex of the chicks before her by employing a highly reliable natural cognitive ability, but who lacks any good reflectively accessible grounds in favour of her beliefs so formed.[26] Here we have an agent who at least potentially has knowledge by epistemic externalist lights (ultimately, whether she does have knowledge will depend on the details of the specific epistemic externalist proposal under consideration), but who is clearly not in a position to properly assert what she knows—much less explicitly assert that she knows it—since she lacks any good reflectively accessible grounds to back up that assertion. If the epistemic externalist neo-Moorean is right in thinking that we can know the denials of radical sceptical hypotheses even though we lack good reflectively accessible grounds in support of our beliefs in this regard, then one's anti-sceptical knowledge will be akin to the 'brute' knowledge possessed by our chicken sexer. On this view, then, it is little wonder that Moore cannot properly make the assertions he does, even when what he asserts is true.

While all epistemic internalist versions of neo-Mooreanism face the problem of explaining why the Moorean anti-sceptical assertions are problematic, epistemological disjunctivist neo-Mooreanism faces a particular problem on this score. For according to this view one possesses not just good reflectively accessible rational support for one's anti-sceptical beliefs, but specifically *factive* reflectively accessible rational support. As a consequence, it is especially hard on this view to understand why assertions of the relevant propositions should be so conversationally inappropriate. It is thus not surprising that McDowell wishes to distance his anti-scepticism from views which try to *answer* the sceptical challenge, and which thereby find themselves making Moorean assertions.

Still, I think that McDowell can be bolder in his treatment of radical scepticism, since, as we will see, there is an intermediate form of anti-scepticism available here, one which answers the radical sceptical argument but which does not do so by making Moorean assertions. What epistemological disjunctivism neo-Mooreanism requires, I suggest, is an account of why such Moorean assertions are inappropriate even though true, an account which is in the spirit of the general tenor of epistemological disjunctivism.

§8. Knowing and Saying That One Knows

Call assertions of the form 'I know that p', where no further caveat is applied to the assertion, *explicit knowledge claims*. To begin with, it is important to note that one rarely conveys one's knowledge by making explicit knowledge claims. Instead, one typically conveys one's knowledge of a proposition simply by asserting the proposition in question. For example, in normal circumstances one might represent oneself as having knowledge of which creature is in the zoo enclosure before one by simply asserting, 'It's a zebra'.[27] But since one can normally convey that one has knowledge of a certain proposition without making an explicit knowledge claim regarding that proposition, one would usually need a special reason for making the logically stronger assertion. This is one reason why explicit knowledge claims are relatively rare, even though we clearly do regularly represent ourselves as having knowledge.

What would prompt an agent to move from the logically weaker non-explicit knowledge claim (i.e., 'It's a zebra') to the corresponding explicit knowledge claim (i.e., 'I know that it's a zebra')? Perhaps the most obvious motivation for making an explicit knowledge claim is to respond to a particular challenge that has been raised regarding one's initial assertion. Since our interest in explicit knowledge claims is precisely in the conditions that govern their propriety in conversational contexts where challenges have been raised (e.g., sceptical challenges), it makes sense for us to focus on this particular motivation for explicit knowledge claims. Moreover, to keep our discussion manageable we will concern ourselves only with those cases where the initial assertion is specifically concerned with a proposition which the agent believes via perception.[28]

So, for example, one might initially convey one's knowledge of what creature is in the zoo enclosure by simply asserting, 'It's a zebra', but then be prompted into the further explicit knowledge claim by a challenge to one's original assertion. The usual way to challenge such an assertion is to raise an error-possibility which is held to be salient. In this case, for instance, it could be that someone raises the possibility that the creature in question might be a cleverly disguised mule, perhaps on the grounds that she'd heard an official from the zoo say that cleverly disguised mules have recently been introduced to the zebra enclosure in order to cut costs (after all, most zoo visitors can't tell the difference anyway).

In responding to a challenge of this sort with an explicit knowledge claim one is representing oneself as being in possession of stronger reflectively accessible grounds in support of one's assertion than would be implied simply by making the assertion itself. It may, for example, be legitimate to support one's original assertion that one can appeal to what it says on the sign above the enclosure (i.e., 'ZEBRAS'). But clearly this wouldn't suffice to rationally support the logically stronger assertion, since the challenger is not disputing that the creature in question is in the (clearly marked) zebra enclosure.

Notice, moreover, that in entering an explicit knowledge claim in response to a challenge involving a specific error-possibility one is not only representing oneself as having stronger reflectively accessible grounds in support of that assertion than would (normally) be required in order to simply assert the target proposition, but also usually representing oneself as being in possession of reflectively accessible grounds which speak *specifically* to the error-possibility raised.[29] In particular—and this is a point which, I think, has often been overlooked in this regard, despite its epistemic importance—the grounds one needs available to one when making an explicit knowledge claim in response to a challenge involving a specific error-possibility must usually be such as to indicate that one can perceptually *discriminate* between the (objects in the) scenario at issue in what is asserted and the relevant error-possibility (at least within the circumstances that one finds oneself in). This claim is important because, as we saw in part two, the kind of evidential support one needs in order to have knowledge, including knowledge by epistemic internalist lights, is often weaker than this. In particular, sometimes all that is required is evidence which *favours* the target proposition over the relevant alternatives.

In order to make this point clear, consider again the 'Zula' example from part two. We noted that Zula, if unaware of any grounds for doubt anyway, would normally count as knowing that there is a zebra before her.

Suppose that she asserts in this conversational context that there is a zebra before her, thereby representing herself as having knowledge of this proposition. We would surely regard such an assertion as proper, not only because it is true but also because Zula has adequate reflectively accessible grounds to back up that assertion. Indeed, if we adopt an epistemological disjunctivist reading of the scenario, then Zula is in possession of factive reflectively accessible rational support, in that she sees that there is a zebra before her.

The question that now concerns us is whether Zula can legitimately respond to a challenge to her initial assertion by making the relevant explicit knowledge claim. As we will see, whether this is so very much depends on the particular conversational circumstances she is in, and in particular on the kind of challenge that she is responding to when making her explicit knowledge claim. There are three main types of case that we should delineate in this regard. The first type is where Zula is confronted by a challenge which does not consist in the presentation of a specific error-possibility. Call this a *bare challenge*. The second type is where Zula is confronted by a challenge which consists in the presentation of a specific error-possibility, but where no epistemic grounds (or at least inadequate epistemic grounds) are offered in support of that error-possibility. Call this an *unmotivated specific challenge*. Finally, the third type is where Zula is confronted by a challenge which consists in the presentation of a specific error-possibility, and where a good epistemic basis is offered in support of that error-possibility. Call this a *motivated specific challenge*.

We will begin by looking at motivated specific challenges, which I take to be the normal way in which an assertion is challenged (for one thing, it is surely part of the basic etiquette of most conversational exchanges that one should only challenge an assertion when one has good reason to do so). Indeed, we have already considered an example of this sort, since the case described above regarding the challenger who offers good grounds for thinking that the creatures in the zebra enclosure might well be cleverly disguised mules instead fits into this template. We noted above that in order to properly respond to this challenge with an explicit claim to know one needed very specific epistemic support.

Imagine now that it is our hero Zula who is confronted with this motivated specific challenge. What would it take for Zula to properly enter an explicit claim to know? Well, merely having good grounds for believing that the creatures in the zebra enclosure really are zebras may not suffice, since such grounds might not speak to the specific error-possibility raised. As noted above, that Zula's reason for thinking that the creature in question is a zebra is that it is in the clearly marked zebra enclosure will not suffice, even though it may have sufficed to ensure that the original assertion was appropriate. This is because the challenger is not disputing that this creature is in the zebra enclosure, but rather offering grounds for thinking that not every creature in the zebra enclosure is a zebra.

So if the only grounds that Zula has available to her are of this limited sort, such that they do not speak to the motivated error-possibility in question, then the situation is one in which she has been presented with a defeater which she cannot in turn defeat. One immediate consequence of this fact is that Zula no longer knows the target proposition, and hence were she to enter the relevant explicit knowledge claim then she would be asserting something false (even worse, asserting something which she is aware, or at least ought to be aware, is false). Making false assertions— especially assertions which one is aware, or ought to be aware, are false—is obviously conversationally inappropriate, but I want to focus on a particular feature of such an explicit knowledge claim which would be problematic. For notice that in entering such an explicit knowledge claim Zula would clearly be falsely representing herself as having an epistemic basis for her belief in the proposition asserted which spoke to the specific error-possibility in question. That is, this assertion would generate the false conversational implicature that she possesses an epistemic basis for her belief in the proposition asserted which speaks to the specific error-possibility in question. As such, such an assertion—even if it were true— would be conversationally inappropriate.[30]

Indeed, even having grounds which do speak to the specific error-possibility raised may not be enough for Zula to properly enter an explicit knowledge claim (even though it would suffice for her to defeat the defeater, and hence retain her knowledge of the target proposition). For suppose that Zula had good reason for thinking that the challenger misunderstood what the zoo official had said (e.g., perhaps Zula was paying more attention than her challenger, and she heard the official specifically say that it was a very specific—and different—enclosure that the cleverly disguised mules had recently been introduced to). Zula might thus have adequate favouring grounds with regard to the asserted proposition (i.e., that the creature is a zebra) as opposed to the target error-possibility (i.e., that the creature is a cleverly disguised mule). But having epistemic support of this favouring sort is entirely compatible with Zula being unable to perceptually discriminate between zebras and cleverly disguised mules, and yet an appropriate explicit knowledge claim—which, recall, is unqualified—in this context seems to demand precisely such a discriminatory capacity.

In order to see this, imagine that Zula, while possessing the favouring epistemic support just noted, is aware that she is unable to perceptually discriminate between cleverly disguised mules and zebras, and yet nonetheless responds to the motivated specific challenge in question by making the relevant explicit knowledge claim. Wouldn't such an assertion seem entirely inappropriate? The reason why such an assertion would be inappropriate, I suggest, is that given the conversational context that Zula is in such an assertion would generate the conversational implicature that she is able (at least in the circumstances she finds herself in anyway) to perceptually discriminate between zebras and cleverly disguised mules. Since she cannot do this, her assertion thus generates a false conversational implicature, and is thus to that extent inappropriate (even though what she asserts—*viz.*, that she knows that the creature is a zebra—is true).

If Zula lacks such a discriminatory capacity, and yet wishes to respond to this challenge with a claim to know, then she will need to qualify her assertion in such a way as to make clear that she is not representing herself as having such a capacity. Zula might thus claim something like this: 'While I can't tell zebras and cleverly disguised mules apart, I know that that's a zebra because I heard the zoo official say that the cleverly disguised mules have been put in a different enclosure.' An assertion of this sort, while still logically stronger than the original assertion (since it involves a claim to know), falls short of an explicit knowledge claim in that it expressly cancels the false conversational implicature that would be generated by an explicit knowledge claim in this case.

Interestingly, what goes for Zula when faced with a motivated specific challenge also applies in the case of an unmotivated specific challenge. For suppose that the very same error-possibility is raised regarding the possibility that the creatures Zula is faced with are in fact cleverly disguised mules, except that now no epistemic basis (or at least an inadequate epistemic basis anyway) is offered in support of this error-possibility. Perhaps, say, someone just wonders out loud in Zula's presence whether these creatures are cleverly disguised mules.

We noted in part two that even where an error-possibility is unmotivated in this way, it is still rationally incumbent upon the agent to be in a position to adduce sufficient favouring epistemic support to neutralize this error-possibility if she is to retain her knowledge in the target proposition. Merely being in possession of such favouring epistemic support will not suffice for Zula to enter the relevant explicit knowledge claim, however, even despite the fact that the error-possibility in question is unmotivated (and even despite the fact that such an assertion would be true).

The reason for this is that given that the error-possibility in question has been raised in that conversational context (even though in an unmotivated fashion), were Zula to enter the relevant explicit knowledge claim this would carry the conversational implicature that she could perceptually discriminate between zebras and cleverly disguised mules. For suppose that Zula were to enter the relevant explicit knowledge claim in this conversational context, where the 'cleverly disguised mule' error-possibility is at issue. Wouldn't one take Zula to be thereby representing herself as being able to perceptually discriminate between zebras and cleverly disguised mules? Accordingly, if Zula is aware that she lacks such discriminatory powers, then (just as in the case of a motivated specific challenge) she should at most assert a qualified claim to know which cancels the relevant conversational implicature.

Note that this is not to deny that the raising of unmotivated challenges is usually conversationally illegitimate, and so the kind of thing that someone like Zula, so challenged, might herself query. Zula might, for example, question the challenger's motivation for making this particular challenge, and reasonably so, given the circumstances surrounding the challenge. But the point is just that if Zula wishes to respond to such a challenge with an explicit claim to know—which is what the challenge in effect invites her to do—then she needs to be confident that she is in possession of the relevant discriminatory capacities.

Moreover, notice that even if we conceive of Zula as being in possession of factive rational support for her belief in the target proposition of the kind advanced by epistemological disjunctivism, this will not make a difference in this regard. We noted in part two that if Zula's epistemic basis for her belief in the target proposition is that she sees that there is a zebra, then such factive epistemic support can suffice to defeat an epistemically unmotivated error-possibility, even though it might not constitute independent grounds against this error-possibility (i.e., even though this epistemic basis is itself called into question by the error-possibility in play). Zula can thus rationally dismiss an unmotivated error-possibility merely by reflecting on the nature of the factive epistemic support available to her, and hence retain her knowledge of the target proposition even with this error-possibility in play.

Unfortunately, that Zula by epistemological disjunctivist lights has such a straightforward way available to her of rationally dismissing unmotivated error-possibilities does not give her any special advantage when it comes to entering explicit knowledge claims. For as we have argued above, entering an explicit knowledge claim in light of any challenge, whether motivated or unmotivated, carries the conversational implicature that the agent making the assertion has the relevant discriminatory powers. Since possessing factive epistemic support only guarantees you favouring epistemic support, it will not follow from the fact that Zula can rationally dismiss this error-possibility that she can thereby appropriately make the explicit knowledge claim. Indeed, one would ordinarily expect that she wouldn't be able to appropriately enter this explicit knowledge claim, since Zula, *qua* layperson, presumably cannot perceptually discriminate between zebras and cleverly disguised mules (and will be aware of this fact), and hence her assertion would generate a false conversational implicature. At most, then, Zula can in this case only assert the 'hedged' claim to know which cancels the relevant conversational implicature.

That leaves bare challenges. Interestingly, they make very different epistemic demands on the subject than the other two challenges. Here is an example of a bare challenge to Zula's initial assertion. Perhaps, for example, this assertion is challenged by someone who—rather rudely— simply disputes it without offering any epistemic basis for doing so. In particular, it is not that the challenger disputes the initial assertion by appeal to a specific error-possibility (as is the case with both motivated and unmotivated specific challenges).

In contrast to the other two cases we have looked at, when it comes to bare challenges like this it surely would be unproblematic for Zula to respond to this challenge by entering the salient explicit knowledge claim. After all, the challenger has offered no grounds for doubt, and neither has she raised a specific error-possibility within that conversational content which Zula should respond to. If Zula's epistemic basis for the original assertion was adequate, then it ought to be likewise adequate for this logically stronger assertion, since the latter assertion is here playing the role of merely emphasizing what was implicit in the former assertion. That is, given that the challenge is not epistemically motivated and there is no specific error-possibility in play in this conversational context, what Zula is doing when she enters the explicit knowledge claim is just reaffirming, in the context of the bare challenge, her confidence in the epistemic basis she has for her previous assertion. In particular, notice that since there is no specific error-possibility in play, in entering the explicit knowledge claim Zula will not be representing herself as having any special discriminatory powers.

Note that this is not to deny that in practice Zula might well qualify her assertion, and so not offer a bare explicit knowledge claim. Zula might explicitly add, for example, some comment about the epistemic basis for her explicit knowledge claim (e.g., she might cite the perceptual evidence available to her). In doing so, I suggest, Zula is simply extending a conversational courtesy to her challenger which her challenger did not extended to her when she presented a bare challenge to the original assertion.

So Zula can legitimately respond to bare challenges to her initial assertion by entering an explicit knowledge claim, but can normally not do this when the challenge consists of either a motivated or unmotivated specific challenge. The reason for this is that in such cases entering an explicit knowledge claim will generate the (usually) false conversational implicature that Zula can perceptually discriminate between zebras and cleverly disguised mules. With all this in mind, we now need to return to see what this tells us about how Zula can respond in the particular challenge posed by radical scepticism.

As we noted in part two, when it comes to radical sceptical error-possibilities, unlike 'local' error-possibilities (e.g., the 'cleverly disguised mule' hypothesis), the problem with regard to being able to perceptually discriminate the target scenarios moves from one of being in degree to one of being in kind. If Zula had been better trained, for example, then she could have been in an epistemic position such that she could perceptually discriminate between zebras and cleverly disguised mules. But there is no sense at all in which Zula could enhance her discriminative powers such that she could perceptually discriminate between a normal scenario and a radical sceptical scenario. There is, after all, nothing that Zula could do which could enable her to perceptually discriminate between the experience as of seeing a zebra and the experience generated by the vat as of seeing a zebra.

We noted above that radical sceptical error-possibilities are in their nature epistemically ungrounded, and that this has an important bearing when it comes to the question of whether, by epistemological disjunctivist lights anyway, one can legitimately dismiss them. Given what we have just argued regarding unmotivated specific challenges, however, this conclusion is of little help when it comes to the salient explicit knowledge claims. For while the epistemological disjunctivist can argue that Zula's knowledge is typically unharmed by the presentation of the sceptical error-possibility, it does not follow that she can make the relevant explicit knowledge claim. That assertion would, after all, require Zula to possess discriminatory capacities that she simply cannot possess. Such an assertion is thus in its nature conversationally inappropriate, since it unavoidably generates a false conversational implicature.

We noted above that provided that the agent concerned was (only) in possession of adequate favouring epistemic support for her belief in the target proposition, then although she couldn't make the relevant explicit knowledge claim she could nonetheless enter a 'hedged' version of this claim which cancelled the conversational implicature in play. Does this point hold in the radical sceptical case? Indeed it does, though as we will see there are some details here that need to be spelled out.

On the face of it, the idea of simply making a 'hedged' knowledge claim doesn't look promising in this case. Consider, for example, the following claim in response to a radical sceptical challenge: 'Look, I can't tell that I'm not a handless BIV, but I *know* that I've got two hands.' Isn't there something very odd even about this qualified knowledge claim?[31]

Indeed there is, but the problem doesn't lie in the assertion as such but in whom we are imagining saying it. For notice that if this claim is made by the epistemological disjunctivist neo-Moorean, then it makes perfect sense, since she *does* have a story in hand about why the target knowledge is possessed even though, by her own admission, she can't offer the relevant discriminatory rational support. In contrast, were someone who is not in possession of this supporting epistemological theory to make this assertion, then we would indeed quite rightly find it problematic. For while, as argued in part two, we do in our epistemological concepts work with a distinction between favouring and discriminating epistemic support, such that (as we have just claimed) we can make sense of why Zula can cancel the implicature that she can discriminate zebras from cleverly disguised mules when she claims to know that what she is looking at is a zebra, the application of this distinction to the radical sceptical case requires some philosophical work and, in particular, the setting of this distinction within a defence of epistemological disjunctivism. Only with that philosophical work done does it really make sense to make an assertion like this.

So once one reflects on the kind of commitments that are incurred when one enters an explicit knowledge claim, and the conversational context in which such conversational moves take place, then it becomes clear that the Moorean assertions can be both conversationally inappropriate and yet entirely true. Epistemological disjunctivist neo-Mooreanism can thus dispel any lingering concerns about their anti-sceptical strategy which arise out of the awkwardness of Moorean anti-sceptical assertions.

§9. Concluding Remarks

In part three we have seen that epistemological disjunctivism can be successfully applied to the problem of radical scepticism, at least provided one embeds the view within some key wider claims. The anti-sceptical position that results is a form of neo-Mooreanism, albeit one that has important advantages over other neo-Moorean views that are cast along epistemic externalist or standard epistemic internalist lines.

A crucial move that we made in arguing for this position was to show that radical sceptical challenges are by their nature unmotivated, where this has a significant effect on the dialectical obligations incurred by the anti-sceptic. In particular, this means that the epistemological disjunctivist neo-Moorean is spared the impossible task of trying to demonstrate that agents have an independent reflectively accessible rational basis for excluding radical sceptical hypotheses. As a result, the path is cleared for this proposal to show how our knowledge of the denials of radical sceptical hypotheses could be supported by reflectively accessible factive reasons.

Moreover, we argued that it was important to the success of the epistemological disjunctivist neo-Moorean position that it be understood as an undercutting, rather than overriding, anti-sceptical strategy. This feature of the view gives it a critical dialectical edge over competing proposals and also ensures that the proposal is intellectually satisfying as a treatment of the problem of radical scepticism.

Finally, we argued that this approach to the radical sceptical problem is able to accommodate the fact that Moorean anti-sceptical assertions are clearly conversationally inappropriate. In doing so, we removed one key spur for taking a quietistic approach to radical scepticism.

This application of epistemological disjunctivism to the problem of radical scepticism is crucial to demonstrating the philosophical potential of this proposal. As we have progressed through this book we have witnessed a transformation in the fortunes of epistemological disjunctivism. At the outset it was merely a view that would be desirable if only it were available. By the end of part two it had transformed into being a position which clearly is available, in that the key problems facing it had been shown to be illusory. And now, at the end of the book, we have seen that this proposal can be put to work to deal with one of the most formidable problems in epistemology. Far from being a lost cause, epistemological disjunctivism turns out to be a proposal which has much to recommend it.

Notes to Part Three

1. Henceforth, unless otherwise indicated I shall take it as given that we are dealing with 'rationally articulate' agents.

2. For a comprehensive overview of recent work on the problem of radical scepticism, see Pritchard (2002b). For specific discussion of the structure of radical sceptical arguments, see Pritchard (2005c).

3. For my own part I actually think there is a lot more (if you'll excuse the pun) going on in Moore's writings on radical scepticism than contemporary 'Mooreanism' suggests, but I will not be getting into this exegetical issue since it is Mooreanism, rather than Moore's own nuanced anti-sceptical view, which is my focus here. For Moore's two key writings on radical scepticism, see Moore (1925; 1939). For an overview of some of the exegetical issues in this regard, see Baldwin (1993). For an excellent survey of Moorean anti-sceptical responses, which includes a discussion of some of the contemporary readings of Moore's own view, see Carter (2012).

4. See Pritchard (2007b) for a fairly comprehensive list.

5. See, for example, Wright (2002) for a complaint against Mooreanism of this sort. See also Pryor (2004) on this point. For a helpful critical discussion of this issue, see Neta (2007).

6. Wright (1991) discusses this '*impasse*' objection to Mooreanism, and offers an argument which shows that the second-order scepticism which results collapses into first-order radical scepticism.

7. As Wittgenstein remarks at one point: "Moore's mistake lies in this—countering the assertion that one cannot know that, by saying 'I do know it'" (Wittgenstein 1969, §521). For further discussion of Wittgenstein's treatment of Moorean anti-scepticism in this regard, see Pritchard (2001; 2005d; 2011d).

8. This aversion to revisionism is why standard contextualist anti-sceptical theories, as defended, for example, by DeRose (1995), Lewis (1996), and Cohen (2000), would not count as neo-Moorean proposals, even though they also allow that we can know the denials of radical sceptical hypotheses. This is because the contextualist achieves this by offering a complex and revisionistic philosophical theory about how our use of the term 'knows' is highly context-sensitive. For the neo-Moorean, however, such revisionism is unnecessary, and merely distracts one from offering the straightforward neo-Moorean response to radical scepticism that is both required and available. For more on the relative merits of neo-Moorean and contextualist anti-sceptical theories, see Pritchard (2005a, part one; 2007b).

9. For more on the issue of how to formulate safety, and its connections to anti-luck epistemology, see Pritchard (2002c; 2005a, *passim*; 2005b; 2007a; 2009b; 2013). Other safety-style principles have been advanced by Sainsbury (1997), Williamson (2000a), and Luper (2003).

10. As noted in part one, one might want to qualify the favouring principle in order to accommodate the intuition that not every belief needs to be evidentially grounded in order to be an instance of knowledge. Notice, though, that such an amendment to the principle wouldn't necessarily make any real difference to its ability to generate radical sceptical conclusions. After all, it is surely the case that when it comes to most of our beliefs in empirical propositions that they must be evidentially grounded if they are to count as knowledge, and that they are only evidentially grounded to a degree that would support knowledge provided that such evidence is able to play this 'favouring' role. And since the radical sceptic only needs to call the epistemic status of most of our beliefs in empirical matters into question in order to motivate her sceptical doubt, this weaker construal of the favouring principle would, it seems, serve the radical sceptic's purposes equally well.

11. For similar reasons, a neo-Moorean view which is cast along standard epistemic internalist lines would also be in tension with the evidential transmission principle which we looked at in part two (§3). Recall that according to this principle one's knowledge-sufficient evidence transfers across competent deductions to be knowledge-sufficient evidence for the deduced belief. But that means that if our everyday beliefs are supported by knowledge-sufficient evidence, then our beliefs in the denials of sceptical hypotheses will enjoy this evidential support too. Accordingly, if this brand of neo-Mooreanism is forced to deny that our beliefs in the denials of sceptical hypotheses are evidentially grounded, then that will threaten the evidential basis of our everyday beliefs too.

12. Though see the *dogmatist* and *conservative* proposals offered by, respectively, Pryor (2000) and Wright (2004*a*). It would take me too far afield to discuss these proposals at length here. As I hope will become clear below, however, once we have adequately described the non-standard epistemic internalist neo-Moorean proposal which epistemological disjunctivism makes available to us, then the impetus for defending any form of standard epistemic internalist neo-Mooreanism evaporates. I critically discuss Wright's anti-sceptical proposal in the context of the alternative epistemological disjunctivist account in Pritchard (2009*c*). See also Pritchard (2005*d*; 2011*d*; 2012*b*). For a key discussion of Pryor's anti-sceptical proposal, see Wright (2007).

   A second kind of anti-sceptical proposal which could arguably be construed along standard epistemic internalist neo-Moorean lines is the idea of there being an *abductive* basis for believing that one is not the victim of a radical sceptical hypothesis. For further discussion of this possibility, see Vogel (1990), and the recent exchange on this topic between Vogel (2005) and Fumerton (2005).

13. By a similar line of reasoning, the epistemic externalist neo-Moorean could also argue that their view is not in tension with the evidential transmission principle either (in contrast to a neo-Moorean view which is cast along standard epistemic internalist lines, as I explain in endnote 11 above).

14. Elsewhere I have developed a neo-Moorean response to radical scepticism that runs along classical epistemic externalist lines in this way. See, for example, Pritchard (2005*a*: part one; 2007*b*). One could also regard Williamson's response to radical scepticism as falling under this general category. See especially Williamson (2000*a*, ch. 8; 2000*b*).

15. It is a concern of this sort that lies behind so-called 'metaepistemological' challenges to epistemic externalist anti-sceptical proposals. See, for example, Fumerton (1990) and Stroud (1994).

16. Elsewhere—especially Pritchard (2008*b*)—I have called this view 'McDowellian Neo-Mooreanism' because it shares key features with the approach to the radical sceptical problem put forward by McDowell (e.g., 1982; 1995). Indeed, as I note in the introduction, McDowell's work on disjunctivism is in general the inspiration for epistemological disjunctivism as I describe the view here. Nonetheless, and as I also explain in the introduction, I want my presentation of the view to stand independently of McDowell's writings, partly to avoid exegetical issues and partly in order to make my formulation of the position as clean and to the point as possible. Accordingly, I won't be using this description to describe this anti-sceptical proposal here, though I will at certain key junctures (particularly in §7) remark on how this proposal relates to McDowell's important work on this topic. For a recent critical discussion of 'McDowellian Neo-Mooreanism', see Schönbaumsfeld (2011).

17. If John is unable to undertake a competent deduction of this sort then clearly he is no longer in a position to know that *p* either. Nothing relevant to the problem of radical scepticism follows from this point, however, since we are only interested in whether the sceptic can deprive us normal folk of knowledge, not whether they can deprive half-wits of knowledge. (But note, too, that on the view under discussion these 'half-wits' can have widespread perceptual knowledge prior to becoming aware of the sceptical error-possibility—this is a direct consequence of the two-tiered relevant alternatives account of perceptual knowledge in play—and so the intellectually challenged should not feel too aggrieved by this epistemological proposal; it is much kinder to them than most.)

18. Brueckner (2010) offers a penetrating critical discussion of the merits of what I am here calling the simpleminded version of epistemological disjunctivism neo-Mooreanism (which he groups together with an epistemic externalist variant of this anti-sceptical line which is offered by Williamson (e.g., 2000*a*, ch. 8; 2000*b*)). In effect, his worry about this form of anti-scepticism is that it is

unable to offer us a dialectically effective response to the problem of radical scepticism. I agree. The rest of part three is my attempt to put forward the additional philosophical argument which epistemological disjunctivist neo-Mooreanism needs in order to be at a dialectical advantage when it comes to the problem of radical scepticism.

19. See Wright (1991) for an important discussion of the idea that the radical sceptical problem needs to be understood specifically in terms of a paradox. See also Stroud (1984, *passim*).

20. As Stroud (1984, 82) famously put it, radical scepticism is a paradox because it falls out of 'platitudes' that 'we would all accept' but which are collectively inconsistent.

21. Just consider the problems that Pyrrhonian sceptics famously face on this score, and their 'lived' doubt is not as universal as the doubt we are considering here. For more discussion of this point, see Pritchard (2011*d*; cf. Pritchard 2000).

22. I explore this aspect of the problem of radical scepticism in Pritchard (2014).

23. A very similar way of thinking about these issues is offered by Cassam (2007*a*). He argues that we should re-cast sceptical problems in terms of 'how possible?' questions, and then distinguishes different levels of response to this problem. This is basically equivalent to re-casting the radical sceptical argument into a paradox, as I explain in Pritchard (2009*b*). Moreover, Cassam then goes on to distinguish (amongst other things) between obstacle-overcoming and obstacle-removing anti-sceptical strategies, which is roughly equivalent to our distinction between overriding and undercutting anti-sceptical strategies. For another similar discussion of the dialectical situation with regard to the radical sceptical problem, see Williams (1991, ch. 1).

24. Notice also that this feature of the epistemological disjunctivist response to radical scepticism also explains why it doesn't face some of the problems that we saw facing Mooreanism above (§2). In particular, what the epistemological disjunctivist is offering is clearly something much stronger than a mere draw with the radical sceptic, and hence the *impasse* problem is avoided. Moreover, given that the epistemological disjunctivist is offering an undercutting anti-sceptical strategy which demonstrates that the sceptical problem is not the paradox that it purports to be, the *dialectical impropriety* problem is also dealt with too. Of course, that still leaves the *conversational impropriety* problem, but we will be examining what the epistemological disjunctivist has to say about anti-sceptical claims to know below in §8.

25. Quietism of this sort is of course closely associated with the later work of Wittgenstein (esp. 1953). For a recent discussion by McDowell of Wittgensteinian quietism, see McDowell (2009).

26. For further discussion of the chicken sexer case, see Foley (1987, 168–9), Lewis (1996), Zagzebski (1996, §2.1 and §4.1), Brandom (1998), and Pritchard (2005a, *passim*).

27. One putative explanation of this phenomenon which has been very popular in the recent literature is the knowledge account of assertion. In a nutshell, this holds that one should only assert that *p* when one knows that *p*. See, especially, Williamson (1996b; 2000a, ch. 11). For a useful recent critical discussion of this proposal, see Weiner (2005). I take no view here on whether we should adopt such a proposal (see also endnote 28 below).

28. With these two caveats in play, it should be clear that in what follows I am not trying to offer universal constraints on explicit knowledge claims (much less assertions in general). For a useful survey of the recent literature on assertion, with particular focus on the epistemic requirements for assertion, see Weiner (2007). See also Weiner (2011).

29. Note that I am assuming here, for the sake of simplicity, that when an initial assertion is challenged by appeal to an error-possibility, only a single error-possibility is raised. In practice, of course, there may be more than one error-possibility raised. Nothing hangs on this for our purposes. What is argued for here with regard to cases involving single error-possibilities applies, *mutatis mutandis*, to cases involving multiple error-possibilities.

30. The *locus classicus* for discussions of conversational implicature is, of course, Grice (1989). For a useful critical discussion of this notion, see Travis (1997).

31. One salient issue in this regard is how best to construe the extent to which conversational implicatures can be 'cancellable'—e.g., how 'easy' should such cancellations be? For discussion on this point, see DeRose and Grandy (1999, esp. n13 and n19).

References

Adler, J. (2002). *Belief's Own Ethics*, Cambridge, MA: MIT Press.

Alston, W. P. (1986). 'The Deontological Conception of Epistemic Justification', *Philosophical Perspectives* 2, 257–99.

—— (1988). 'An Internalist Externalism', *Synthese* 74, 265–83.

Austin, J. L. (1961). 'Other Minds', in his *Philosophical Papers*, ed. J. O. Urmson and G. J. Warnock, 76–116, Oxford: Clarendon Press.

Bach, K. (1985). 'A Rationale for Reliabilism', *Monist* 68, 246–63.

Baldwin, T. (1993). 'G. E. Moore', *A Companion to Epistemology*, ed. J. Dancy and E. Sosa, 283–5, Oxford: Blackwell.

Berker, S. (2008). 'Luminosity Regained', *Philosophers' Imprint* 8, 1–22.

Bernecker, S. (2007). 'Remembering Without Knowing', *Australasian Journal of Philosophy* 85, 137–56.

Black, T. (2002). 'A Moorean Response to Brain-In-A-Vat Scepticism', *Australasian Journal of Philosophy* 80, 148–63.

—— (2011). 'Review of *Perception as a Capacity for Knowledge*, by John McDowell', *Notre Dame Philosophical Reviews*, http://ndpr.nd.edu/news/24767/?id=24292

BonJour, L. (1985). *The Structure of Empirical Knowledge*, Cambridge, MA: Harvard University Press.

—— (2002). 'Internalism and Externalism', *Oxford Handbook of Epistemology*, ed. P. Moser, 234–64, Oxford: Oxford University Press.

Brandom, R. (1995). 'Knowledge and the Social Articulation of Reasons', *Philosophy and Phenomenological Research* 55, 889–908.

—— (1998). 'Insights and Blindspots of Reliabilism', *Monist* 81, 371–92.

Brewer, B. (2000). *Perception and Reason*, Oxford: Oxford University Press.

Brogaard, B. (2010). 'Disjunctivism', *Oxford Bibliographies Online: Philosophy*, DOI: 10.1093/OBO/9780195396577-0033.

Brueckner, A. (1994). 'The Structure of the Skeptical Argument', *Philosophy and Phenomenological Research* 54, 827–35.

—— (2010). '¬K¬SK', in his *Essays on Skepticism*, 367–81, Oxford: Oxford University Press.

—— and Fiocco, M. O. (2002). 'Williamson's Anti-Luminosity Argument', *Philosophical Studies* 110, 285–93.

Burge, T. (2003). 'Perceptual Entitlement', *Philosophy and Phenomenological Research* 67, 503–48.

Byrne, A. and Logue, H. (2008). 'Either/Or', *Disjunctivism: Perception, Action, Knowledge*, ed. A. Haddock and F. Macpherson, 57–94, Oxford: Oxford University Press.

————— (eds.) (2009a). *Disjunctivism: Contemporary Readings*, Cambridge, MA: MIT Press.

————— (2009b). 'Introduction', *Disjunctivism: Contemporary Readings*, ed. A. Byrne and H. Logue, vii–xxix, Cambridge, MA: MIT Press.

Carter, J. A. (2012). 'Recent Work on Moore's Proof', *International Journal for the Study of Skepticism* 2, http://www.ingentaconnect.com/content/brill/skep/preprints/skep1034

Cassam, Q. (2007a). *The Possibility of Knowledge*, Oxford: Oxford University Press.

—— (2007b). 'Ways of Knowing', *Proceedings of the Aristotelian Society* 107, 339–58.

Chisholm, R. M. (1977). *Theory of Knowledge* (2nd edn.), Englewood Cliffs, NJ: Prentice-Hall.

Christensen, D. (2010). 'Higher-Order Evidence', *Philosophy and Phenomenological Research* 81, 215–85.

Cohen, S. (1984). 'Justification and Truth', *Philosophical Studies* 46, 279–96.

—— (1988). 'How to be a Fallibilist', *Philosophical Perspectives* 2, 91–123.

—— (1998). 'Two Kinds of Sceptical Argument', *Philosophy and Phenomenological Research* 58, 143–59.

—— (2000). 'Contextualism and Skepticism', *Philosophical Issues* 10, 94–107.

Conee, E. (2007). 'Disjunctivism and Anti-Skepticism', *Philosophical Issues* 17, 16–36.

—— and Feldman, R. (2000). 'Internalism Defended', *Epistemology: Internalism and Externalism*, ed. H. Kornblith, 231–60, Oxford: Blackwell.

————— (2004). *Evidentialism: Essays in Epistemology*, Oxford: Oxford University Press.

————— (2011). 'Reply to Pritchard', *Evidentialism and its Discontents*, ed. T. Dougherty, 440–4, Oxford: Oxford University Press.

Dancy, J. (2008). 'On How to Act—Disjunctively', *Disjunctivism: Perception, Action, Knowledge*, ed. A. Haddock and F. Macpherson, 262–82, Oxford: Oxford University Press.

Davies, M. (2004). 'Epistemic Entitlement, Warrant Transmission and Easy Knowledge', *Proceedings of the Aristotelian Society* 78 (suppl. vol.), 213–45.

DeRose, K. (1995). 'Solving the Skeptical Problem', *Philosophical Review* 104, 1–52.

—— and Grandy, R. (1999). 'Conditional Assertions and "Biscuit" Conditionals', *Noûs* 33, 405–20.

Dorsch, F. (2011). 'The Diversity of Disjunctivism', *European Journal of Philosophy* 19, 304–14.

Dougherty, T. (ed.) (2011). *Evidentialism and its Discontents*, Oxford: Oxford University Press.

Dretske, F. (1969). *Seeing and Knowing*, London: Routledge & Kegan Paul.

—— (1970). 'Epistemic Operators', *Journal of Philosophy* 67, 1007–23.

—— (2005*a*). 'The Case Against Closure', *Contemporary Debates in Epistemology*, ed. E. Sosa and M. Steup, 13–26, Oxford: Blackwell.

—— (2005*b*). 'Reply to Hawthorne', *Contemporary Debates in Epistemology*, ed. E. Sosa and M. Steup, 43–6, Oxford: Blackwell.

Engel, M. (1992). 'Personal and Doxastic Justification', *Philosophical Studies* 67, 133–51.

Fish, W. (2009). 'Disjunctivism', *Internet Encyclopaedia of Philosophy*, ed. B. Dowden and J. Fieser, http://www.iep.utm.edu/d/disjunct.htm

Foley, R. (1987). *A Theory of Epistemic Rationality*, Cambridge, MA: Harvard University Press.

Fumerton, R. (1990). 'Metaepistemology and Skepticism', *Doubting: Contemporary Perspectives on Skepticism*, ed. M. D. Roth and G. Ross, 57–68, Dordrecht: Kluwer.

—— (2005). 'The Challenge of Refuting Skepticism', *Contemporary Debates in Epistemology*, ed. E. Sosa and M. Steup, 85–97, Oxford: Blackwell.

Gendler, T. S. and Hawthorne, J. (2005). 'The Real Guide to Fake Barns: A Catalogue of Gifts for your Epistemic Enemies', *Philosophical Studies* 124, 331–52.

Goldman, A. (1976). 'Discrimination and Perceptual Knowledge', *Journal of Philosophy* 73, 771–91.

—— (1979). 'What Is Justified Belief?', *Justification and Knowledge*, ed. G. Pappas, 1–23, Dordrecht: Reidel.

—— (1986). *Epistemology and Cognition*, Cambridge, MA: Harvard University Press.

—— (1988). 'Strong and Weak Justification', *Philosophical Perspectives 2: Epistemology*, ed. J. Tomberlin, 51–69, Atascadero, CA: Ridgeview.

Greco, J. (2004). 'Externalism and Skepticism', *The Externalist Challenge: New Studies on Cognition and Intentionality*, ed. R. Schantz, 53–64, New York: de Gruyter.

—— (2010). *Achieving Knowledge: A Virtue-Theoretic Account of Epistemic Normativity*, Cambridge: Cambridge University Press.

Grice, H. P. (1961). 'The Causal Theory of Perception', *Proceedings of the Aristotelian Society* (suppl. vol.) 35, 121–52.

—— (1989). 'Logic and Conversation', in his *Studies in the Way of Words*, 22–40, Cambridge, MA: Harvard University Press.

Haddock, A. (2011). 'The Disjunctive Conception of Perceiving', *Philosophical Explorations* 14, 69–88.

—— and Macpherson, F. (eds.) (2008*a*). *Disjunctivism: Perception, Action, Knowledge*, Oxford: Oxford University Press.

Haddock, A. and Macpherson, F. (2008*b*). 'Introduction: Varieties of Disjunctivism', *Disjunctivism: Perception, Action, Knowledge*, ed. A. Haddock and F. Macpherson, 1–24, Oxford: Oxford University Press.

——, Millar, A., and Pritchard, D. H. (eds.) (2010). *Epistemic Value*, Oxford: Oxford University Press.

Halpern, J. Y. (2008). 'Intransitivity and Vagueness', *Review of Symbolic Logic* 1, 530–47.

Hawthorne, J. (2004). *Knowledge and Lotteries*, Oxford: Clarendon Press.

—— (2005). 'The Case for Closure', *Contemporary Debates in Epistemology*, ed. E. Sosa and M. Steup, 26–43, Oxford: Blackwell.

—— and Kovakovich, K. (2006). 'Disjunctivism', *Proceedings of the Aristotelian Society* (suppl. vol.) 80, 145–83.

Hetherington, S. (2013). 'There Can be Lucky Knowledge', *Contemporary Debates in Epistemology* (2nd edn.), ed. M. Steup and J. Turri, 164–76, Oxford: Blackwell.

Hinton, J. M. (1967*a*). 'Experiences', *Philosophical Quarterly* 17, 1–13.

—— (1967*b*). 'Visual Experiences', *Mind* 76, 217–27.

—— (1973). *Experiences: An Inquiry into Some Ambiguities*, Oxford: Clarendon Press.

Hornsby, J. (2008). 'A Disjunctive Conception of Acting for Reasons', *Disjunctivism: Perception, Action, Knowledge*, ed. F. Macpherson and A. Haddock, 244–61, Oxford: Oxford University Press.

Kelp, C. (2011). 'A Problem for Contrastivist Accounts of Knowledge', *Philosophical Studies* 152, 287–92.

Klein, P. (1995). 'Skepticism and Closure: Why the Evil Genius Argument Fails', *Philosophical Topics* 23, 213–36.

Lehrer, K. and Cohen, S. (1983). 'Justification, Truth, and Coherence', *Synthese* 55, 191–207.

Lewis, D. (1973). *Counterfactuals*, Oxford: Blackwell.

—— (1996). 'Elusive Knowledge', *Australasian Journal of Philosophy* 74, 549–67.

Littlejohn, C. (2009). 'The New Evil Demon Problem', *Internet Encyclopaedia of Philosophy*, ed. B. Dowden and J. Fieser, www.iep.utm.edu/evil-new/

Luper, S. (2003). 'Indiscernability Skepticism', *The Skeptics: Contemporary Essays*, ed. S. Luper, 183–202, Aldershot: Ashgate.

Madison, B. (2010). 'Epistemic Internalism', *Philosophy Compass* 5, 840–53.

Martin, M. G. F. (2002). 'The Transparency of Experience', *Mind and Language* 17, 376–425.

—— (2004). 'The Limits of Self-Awareness', *Philosophical Studies* 120, 37–89.

—— (2006). 'On Being Alienated', *Perceptual Experience*, ed. T. S. Gendler and J. Hawthorne, 354–410, Oxford: Oxford University Press.

McDowell, J. (1982). 'Criteria, Defeasibility and Knowledge', *Proceedings of the British Academy* 68, 455–79.

—— (1994). 'Knowledge by Hearsay', *Knowing from Words: Western and Indian Philosophical Analysis of Understanding and Testimony*, ed. B. K. Matilal and A. Chakrabarti, 195–224, Dordrecht: Kluwer.

—— (1995). 'Knowledge and the Internal', *Philosophy and Phenomenological Research* 55, 877–93.

—— (2002a). 'Knowledge and the Internal Revisited', *Philosophy and Phenomenological Research* 64, 97–105.

—— (2002b). 'Responses', *Reading McDowell: On Mind and World*, ed. N. H. Smith, 269–305, London: Routledge.

—— (2003). 'Subjective, Intersubjective, Objective', *Philosophy and Phenomenological Research* 67, 675–81.

—— (2008). 'The Disjunctive Conception of Experience as Material for a Transcendental Argument', *Disjunctivism: Perception, Action, Knowledge*, ed. A. Haddock and F. Macpherson, 376–89, Oxford: Oxford University Press.

—— (2009). 'Wittgenstein's "Quietism"', *Common Knowledge* 15, 365–72.

—— (2011). *Perception as a Capacity for Knowledge*, Milwaukee, WI: Marquette University Press.

McKinsey, M. (1991). 'Anti-Individualism and Privileged Access', *Analysis* 51, 9–16.

Millar, A. (2007). 'What the Disjunctivist is Right About', *Philosophy and Phenomenological Research* 74, 176–98.

—— (2008). 'Perceptual-Recognitional Abilities and Perceptual Knowledge', *Disjunctivism: Perception, Action, Knowledge*, ed. A. Haddock and F. Macpherson, 330–47, Oxford: Oxford University Press.

Moore, G. E. (1925). 'A Defence of Common Sense', *Contemporary British Philosophy* (2nd series), ed. J. H. Muirhead, London: Allen & Unwin.

—— (1939). 'Proof of an External World', *Proceedings of the British Academy* 25, 273–300.

Neta, R. (2007). 'Fixing the Transmission: The Neo-Mooreans', *Themes from G. E. Moore: New Essays in Epistemology and Ethics*, ed. S. Nuccetelli and G. Seay, 62–83, Oxford: Oxford University Press.

—— and Pritchard, D. H. (2007). 'McDowell and the New Evil Genius', *Philosophy and Phenomenological Research* 74, 381–96.

Nozick, R. (1981). *Philosophical Explanations*, Oxford: Oxford University Press.

Nuccetelli, S. (ed.) (2003). *New Essays on Semantic Externalism and Self-Knowledge*, Cambridge, MA: MIT Press.

Pappas, G. (2005). 'Internalist *versus* Externalist Conceptions of Epistemic Justification', *Stanford Encyclopaedia of Philosophy*, ed. E. Zalta, http://plato.stanford.edu/entries/justep-intext/

Plantinga, A. (1986). 'The Foundations of Theism: A Reply', *Faith and Philosophy* 3, 310–12.

Poston, T. (2008). 'Internalism and Externalism in Epistemology', *Internet Encyclopaedia of Philosophy*, ed. B. Dowden and J. Fieser, www.iep.utm.edu/int-ext/

Pritchard, D. H. (2000). 'Doubt Undogmatized: Pyrrhonian Scepticism, Epistemological Externalism, and the "Metaepistemological" Challenge', *Principia—Revista Internacional de Epistemologia* 4, 187–214.

—— (2001). 'Radical Scepticism, Epistemological Externalism, and "Hinge" Propositions', *Wittgenstein-Jahrbuch 2001/2002*, ed. D. Salehi, 97–122, Frankfurt: Peter Lang.

—— (2002*a*). 'Radical Scepticism, Epistemological Externalism, and Closure', *Theoria* 68, 129–61.

—— (2002*b*). 'Recent Work on Radical Skepticism', *American Philosophical Quarterly* 39, 215–57.

—— (2002*c*). 'Resurrecting the Moorean Response to Scepticism', *International Journal of Philosophical Studies* 10, 283–307.

—— (2003). 'McDowell on Reasons, Externalism and Scepticism', *European Journal of Philosophy* 11, 273–94.

—— (2005*a*). *Epistemic Luck*, Oxford: Oxford University Press.

—— (2005*b*). 'Scepticism, Epistemic Luck and Epistemic *Angst*', *Australasian Journal of Philosophy*, 83, 185–206.

—— (2005*c*). 'The Structure of Sceptical Arguments', *Philosophical Quarterly* 55, 37–52.

—— (2005*d*). 'Wittgenstein's *On Certainty* and Contemporary Anti-Scepticism', *Investigating On Certainty: Essays on Wittgenstein's Last Work*, ed. D. Moyal-Sharrock and W. H. Brenner, 189–224, Basingstoke: Palgrave Macmillan.

—— (2007*a*). 'Anti-Luck Epistemology', *Synthese* 158, 277–97.

—— (2007*b*). 'How to be a Neo-Moorean', *Internalism and Externalism in Semantics and Epistemology*, ed. S. Goldberg, 68–99, Oxford: Oxford University Press.

—— (2007*c*). 'Knowledge, Luck, and Lotteries', *New Waves in Epistemology*, ed. V. F. Hendricks and D. H. Pritchard, 28–51, Aldershot: Ashgate.

—— (2008*a*). 'Contrastivism, Evidence, and Scepticism', *Social Epistemology* 22, 305–23.

—— (2008*b*). 'McDowellian Neo-Mooreanism', *Disjunctivism: Perception, Action, Knowledge*, ed. A. Haddock and F. Macpherson, 283–310, Oxford: Oxford University Press.

—— (2008*c*). 'Sensitivity, Safety, and Anti-Luck Epistemology', *The Oxford Handbook of Scepticism*, ed. J. Greco, 437–55, Oxford: Oxford University Press, 2008.

—— (2009*a*). 'Apt Performance and Epistemic Value', *Philosophical Studies* 143, 407–16.

—— (2009*b*). 'Safety-Based Epistemology: Whither Now?', *Journal of Philosophical Research* 34, 33–45.

—— (2009*c*). 'Wright *Contra* McDowell on Perceptual Knowledge and Scepticism', *Synthese* 171, 467–79.

—— (2010). 'Relevant Alternatives, Perceptual Knowledge and Discrimination', *Noûs* 44, 245–68.

—— (2011*a*). 'Epistemological Disjunctivism and the Basis Problem', *Philosophical Issues* 21, 434–55.

—— (2011*b*). 'Evidentialism, Internalism, Disjunctivism', *Evidentialism and its Discontents*, ed. T. Dougherty, 362–92, Oxford: Oxford University Press.

—— (2011*c*). 'Wittgensteinian Pyrrhonism', *Pyrrhonism in Ancient, Modern, and Contemporary Philosophy*, ed. D. Machuca, 193–202, Dordrecht: Springer.

—— (2011*d*). 'Wittgenstein on Scepticism', *The Oxford Handbook on Wittgenstein*, ed. O. Kuusela and M. McGinn, 521–47, Oxford: Oxford University Press.

—— (2012*a*). 'Anti-Luck Virtue Epistemology', *Journal of Philosophy* 109, 247–79.

—— (2012*b*). 'Wittgenstein and the Groundlessness of Our Believing', *Synthese* 189, 255–72.

—— (2013). 'There Cannot be Lucky Knowledge', *Contemporary Debates in Epistemology* (2nd edn.), (eds.) M. Steup, J. Turri, and E. Sosa, 152–163 Oxford: Blackwell.

—— (2014). 'Sceptical Intuitions', *Intuitions*, (eds.) D. Rowbottom and T. Booth, 213–31, Oxford: Oxford University Press.

——, Millar, A., and Haddock, A. (2010). *The Nature and Value of Knowledge: Three Investigations*, Oxford: Oxford University Press.

Pryor, J. (2000). 'The Skeptic and the Dogmatist', *Noûs* 34, 517–49.

—— (2001). 'Highlights of Recent Epistemology', *British Journal for the Philosophy of Science* 52, 95–124.

—— (2004). 'Is Moore's Argument an Example of Transmission Failure?', *Philosophical Issues* 14, 349–78.

Ruben, D. H. (2008). 'Disjunctive Theories of Perception and Action', *Disjunctivism: Perception, Action, Knowledge*, ed. A. Haddock and F. Macpherson, 227–43, Oxford: Oxford University Press.

Sainsbury, R. M. (1997). 'Easy Possibilities', *Philosophy and Phenomenological Research* 57, 907–19.

Schaffer, J. (2005). 'Contrastive Knowledge', *Oxford Studies in Epistemology*, vol. 1, 235–72, ed. T. Gendler and J. Hawthorne, Oxford: Oxford University Press.

—— (2006). 'Closure, Contrast, and Answer', *Philosophical Studies* 133, 233–55.

Schönbaumsfeld, G. (2011). 'McDowellian Neo-Mooreanism?', typescript.

Sinnott-Armstrong, W. (2006). *Moral Skepticisms*, New York: Oxford University Press.

Snowdon, P. (1980–1). 'Perception, Vision and Causation', *Proceedings of the Aristotelian Society* (new series) 81, 175–92.

—— (1990–1). 'The Objects of Perceptual Experience', *Proceedings of the Aristotelian Society* (suppl. vol.) 64, 121–50.

—— (2005). 'The Formulation of Disjunctivism: A Response to Fish', *Proceedings of the Aristotelian Society* 105, 129–41.

Sosa, E. (1999). 'How to Defeat Opposition to Moore', *Philosophical Perspectives* 13, 141–54.

—— (2000). 'Skepticism and Contextualism', *Philosophical Issues* 10, 1–18.

—— (2003). *Epistemic Justification: Internalism vs. Externalism, Foundations vs. Virtues*, Oxford: Blackwell.

—— (2007). *A Virtue Epistemology: Apt Belief and Reflective Knowledge*, Oxford: Oxford University Press.

Soteriou, M. (2009). 'The Disjunctive Theory of Perception', *Stanford Encyclopaedia of Philosophy*, ed. E. Zalta, http://plato.stanford.edu/entries/perception-disjunctive/

Stalnaker, R. (1968). 'A Theory of Conditionals', *Studies in Logical Theory*, ed. N. Rescher, 98–112, Oxford: Blackwell.

Stanley, J. (2005). *Knowledge and Practical Interests*, Oxford: Clarendon Press.

Steup, M. (1999). 'A Defense of Internalism', *The Theory of Knowledge: Classical and Contemporary Readings* (3rd edn.), ed. L. Pojman, 310–21, Belmont, CA: Wadsworth.

—— (2009). 'Are Mental States Luminous?', *Williamson on Knowledge*, ed. P. Greenough and D. H. Pritchard, 217–36, Oxford: Oxford University Press.

Stine, G. (1976). 'Skepticism, Relevant Alternatives, and Deductive Closure', *Philosophical Studies* 29, 249–61.

Strawson, P. F. (1974). 'Causation in Perception', in his *Freedom and Resentment*, 73–93, London: Methuen.

Stroud, B. (1984). *The Significance of Philosophical Scepticism*, Oxford: Clarendon Press.

—— (1994). 'Scepticism, "Externalism", and the Goal of Epistemology', *Proceedings of the Aristotelian Society* (suppl. vol.) 68, 290–307.

—— (2002). 'Sense-Experience and the Grounding of Thought', *Reading McDowell: On Mind and World*, ed. N. H. Smith, 79–91, London: Routledge.

Sturgeon, S. (2006). 'Reflective Disjunctivism', *Proceedings of the Aristotelian Society* (suppl. vol.) 80, 185–216.

Tennant, N. (2009). 'Cognitive Phenomenology, Semantic Qualia', *Williamson on Knowledge*, ed. P. Greenough and D. H. Pritchard, 237–56, Oxford: Oxford University Press.

Travis, C. (1997). 'Pragmatics', *A Companion to the Philosophy of Language*, ed. B. Hale and C. J. G. Wright, 87–107, Oxford: Blackwell.

Turri, J. (2010). 'Does Perceiving Entail Knowing?', *Theoria* 76, 197–206.

Unger, P. (1968). 'An Analysis of Factual Knowledge', *Journal of Philosophy* 65, 157–70.

Vogel, J. (1990). 'Cartesian Skepticism and Inference to the Best Explanation', *Journal of Philosophy* 87, 658–66.

—— (2004). 'Skeptical Arguments', *Philosophical Issues* 14, 426–55.

—— (2005). 'The Refutation of Skepticism', *Contemporary Debates in Epistemology*, ed. E. Sosa and M. Steup, 72–84, Oxford: Blackwell.

Weiner, M. (2005). 'Must We Know What We Say?', *Philosophical Review* 114, 227–51.

—— (2007). 'Norms of Assertion', *Philosophy Compass* 2, 187–95.

—— (2011). 'Assertion', *Oxford Bibliographies Online: Philosophy*, DOI: 10.1093/ OBO/9780195396577-0148.

Williams, M. (1991). *Unnatural Doubts: Epistemological Realism and the Basis of Scepticism*, Oxford: Blackwell.

Williamson, T. (1995). 'Is Knowledge a State of Mind?', *Mind* 104, 533–65.

—— (1996a). 'Cognitive Homelessness', *Journal of Philosophy* 93, 554–73.

—— (1996b). 'Knowing and Asserting', *Philosophical Review* 105, 489–523.

—— (2000a). *Knowledge and its Limits*, Oxford: Oxford University Press.

—— (2000b). 'Scepticism and Evidence', *Philosophy and Phenomenological Research* 60, 613–28.

—— (2009). 'Replies to My Critics', *Williamson on Knowledge*, ed. P. Greenough and D. H. Pritchard, 279–384, Oxford: Oxford University Press.

Wittgenstein, L. (1953). *Philosophical Investigations*, ed. G. E. M. Anscombe and R. Rhees, trans. G. E. M. Anscombe, Oxford: Blackwell.

—— (1969). *On Certainty*, ed. G. E. M. Anscombe and G. H. von Wright, trans. D. Paul and G. E. M. Anscombe, Oxford: Blackwell.

Wright, C. J. G. (1991). 'Scepticism and Dreaming: Imploding the Demon', *Mind* 397, 87–115.

—— (1996). 'Human Nature?', *European Journal of Philosophy* 4, 235–53.

—— (2002). '(Anti-)Skeptics Simple and Subtle: G. E. Moore and John McDowell', *Philosophy and Phenomenological Research* 65, 330–48.

—— (2003a). 'Some Reflections on the Acquisition of Warrant by Inference', *New Essays on Semantic Externalism and Self-Knowledge*, ed. S. Nuccetelli, 57–78, Cambridge, MA: MIT Press.

—— (2004a). 'Warrant for Nothing (and Foundations for Free)?', *Proceedings of the Aristotelian Society* (suppl. vol.) 78, 167–212.

—— (2007). 'The Perils of Dogmatism', *Themes from G. E. Moore: New Essays in Epistemology and Ethics*, ed. S. Nuccetelli and G. Seay, 25–48, Oxford: Oxford University Press.

Yalçin, Ü. (1992). 'Sceptical Arguments from Underdetermination', *Philosophical Studies* 68, 1–34.

Zagzebski, L. (1996). *Virtues of the Mind: An Inquiry into the Nature of Virtue and the Ethical Foundations of Knowledge*, Cambridge: Cambridge University Press.

Index

Lightning Source UK Ltd.
Milton Keynes UK
UKOW05f2327240315

248417UK00004BA/9/P